TELEVISION in AMERICA

The SAGE CommText Series

Editor:
F. GERALD KLINE
Director, School of Journalism and Mass Communication
University of Minnesota

Associate Editor:
SUSAN H. EVANS
Department of Communication, University of Michigan

This new series of communication textbooks is designed to provide a modular approach to teaching in this rapidly changing area. The explosion of concepts, methodologies, levels of analysis, and philosophical perspectives has put heavy demands on teaching undergraduates and graduates alike; it is our intent to choose the most solidly argued of these to make them available for students and teachers. The addition of new titles in the COMMTEXT series as well as the presentation of new and diverse authors will be a continuing effort on our part to reflect change in this scholarly area.

—F.G.K. and S.H.E.

Available in this series:

1. TELEVISION IN AMERICA
   George Comstock
2. COMMUNICATION HISTORY
   John D. Stevens and Hazel Dicken Garcia
3. PRIME-TIME TELEVISION: Content and Control
   Muriel G. Cantor
4. MOVIES AS MASS COMMUNICATION
   Garth Jowett and James M. Linton
5. CONTENT ANALYSIS: An Introduction to Its Methodology
   Klaus Krippendorff

additional titles in preparation

George Comstock

TELEVISION
in
AMERICA

Volume 1. **The Sage COMMTEXT Series**

SAGE PUBLICATIONS   Beverly Hills   London

1980

FOR

JACQUELINE FAYE VINCENT

Copyright © 1980 by Sage Publications, Inc.

For information address:

SAGE Publications, Inc.
275 South Beverly Drive
Beverly Hills, California 90212

SAGE Publications Ltd
28 Banner Street
London EC1Y 8QE, England

Printed in the United States of America

Library of Congress Cataloging in Publication Data

Comstock, George A.
    Television in America.

    (Sage commtext ; v. 1)
    Bibliography: p.
    1. Television broadcasting—United States.
I. Title. II. Series.
HE8700.8.C654   384.55'4'0973   80-10891
ISBN 0-8039-1244-7
ISBN 0-8039-1245-5 pbk.

THIRD PRINTING

CONTENTS

ACKNOWLEDGMENTS

This work owes much to the author's previous writings and thus to the persons whose help made them possible: Steven Chaffee, Robin E. Cobbey, Marilyn Fisher, Natan Katzman, Maxwell McCombs, Donald Roberts, and Eli A. Rubinstein. Two careful readers, Ann Rogers and Stacy Veeder, have protected the author from injustices to diction and syntax. Henry F. Schulte, as Dean of the S.I. Newhouse School of Public Communications at Syracuse University, provided an absolutely essential element—an environment amenable to its writing.

Portions of this volume in a different form have appeared as articles in the *Journal of Communication* and in papers commissioned or invited by Action for Children's Television; the Center for Afro-American Studies at the University of California, Los Angeles; the East-West Communication Institute at Honolulu; the Educational Resources Information Center (ERIC) at Syracuse University; the Ford Foundation; and the National Institute of Mental Health. Grateful acknowledgment is extended for the encouragement and support of these parties, none of which bears any responsibility for what is said.

AUTHOR'S PREFACE

This brief volume is a broad and, I hope, provocative analysis of what the study of psychology, political behavior, broadcasting, sociology, and communications tells us about television in the United States. The shifts from empirical evidence to theory to speculation are clear and intentional.

The research is largely treated by genre, thrust, and school of thought. Only major figures, the authors of particularly important works, and those of works which are particularly intriguing—a status often associated with recency of appearance—are named, and the items likely to be of interest to the reader can be found at the end. There is no comprehensive body of citations and no bibliography beyond these recommendations.

The theme of this book is that television is neither simply entertainment nor, for some hours, simply news, but an institution that is some of both at all times and, for that reason, influences our lives. It achieves this influence by the time it consumes, by the incursion of that time on other activities and competing media, and by the content of what it disseminates. The content, in turn, is the product of the medium's economic character and social role. The study of this institution has provided confirmation for some suppositions and disconfirmation for others, and such formal evidence is the foundation for everything that is said. However, it would be foolish to pretend that "research," given the resources that have been devoted to any particular question, will consistently reply with compelling, definitive answers, or that there are not some questions difficult or impossible to confront directly in any sound way by available methods and techniques. We should not be afraid that empirical evidence will mislead us as much as we should be careful that we do not discard what it can tell us by subjecting it to unrealistic or inconsistent standards. The broadcasting and advertising businesses—the "industry"—naturally apply very harsh criteria when they find results unpleasant, and quite different criteria when they seek guidance toward their own ends, as in program testing and advertising evaluation. We should not be so silly.

A laboratory-type experiment may produce results that, by themselves, are limited in their generalizability to everyday events. For that reason, we should look for other evidence that confirms or modifies the conclusion to which the experimental results would seem to lead. However, we should also be imaginative enough to ask ourselves what kind of evidence we might ask for were that or other experiments not available—for we might discover that the answers we disdain are precisely those we ourselves would have sought.

The same applies to the results of surveys, studies of broadcasting organizations, and other investigations limited in population and scope. Obviously, they are subject to the criticism that what they have to say might not apply more broadly. We should not throw them aside for this reason, but instead should ask ourselves just how different elsewhere, and why, we might expect things to be given what the study in question tells us.

When we combine empirical findings with the theories which they have helped shape, we are able to say much more that is meaningful than when we do not go beyond the so-called hard evidence. These theories, because they have been shaped by empirical investigation and because many of the predictions to which they lead have been empirically confirmed, are not simply speculation, but plausible, fact-rooted interpretations of events and behavior that give us some understanding of what research has not specifically encompassed, including the future. Speculation is a further step toward embracing larger and more elusive questions that do not fall clearly within the net of either empiricism or theory, but is far from guesswork because it draws on these bases. The heart of this volume is the confluence of these modes of thinking—empiricism, theory, and its extrapolation beyond what has received substantial support.

—G. C.

1

NOT SO COOL

American television can be described in three words—nonpaternalism, entertainment, and competition. These are terms that are two-edged. What they imply for praise or condemnation, reform or protection of the status quo, depends on the perspective of the speaker and the consequent shape he gives to the facts.

NONPATERNALISM

Broadcasting in the United States is the creature of federal regulation. Its character derives from the conditions to which it responds, and these are largely the product of policies adopted by the federal government. These policies, proclaimed in legislation, applied over the past decades by the Federal Communications Commission (FCC) and the Federal Trade Commission (FTC) and continually dulled or sharpened by the mood of the current Congress, are responsible for the number of television stations, the relative strengths of public and commercial broadcasting, and the way both kinds of stations behave. It is a circuitous journey from federal statute to last night's television programming, and one in which the traveler will be as astounded as Gulliver, but it is the path of insight.

The fulcrum for the federal role is the principle of obligation in exchange for privilege. The privilege, in this case, is economic in the form of the license that permits a television station to operate. The value of a commercial station depends not upon the equipment it possesses, which, like a used car, certainly will bring some return in the marketplace, but upon the flow of income made possible by its broadcasting license. Behind licensing is the belief that the resources of a given community can be equitably and properly mined by a selected few.

Obviously, there is for television and radio stations (as for newspapers) a limit on the number that a particular community can support. Licensing imposes a further restriction on the stations that can operate within a geographical area. No such artificial limitation holds for newspapers or magazines, and thus we have come to treat broadcast media differently from print media.

Television stations are licensed to ensure that signals will not conflict. A condition for the license required, in the language of the Federal Communications Act of 1934, is that the station must serve the "public interest, convenience, and necessity." To justify such behavior, the airwaves are designated as public property. It could just as easily be said, and many regularly do, that because the airwaves *are* public, licenses are imposed and service required. In principle, the purpose of regulation is to ensure that the chaos that might result from open competition does not interfere with the delivery of service to the public.

Because of the very high demand for commercial time on the part of advertisers, the limitation of licenses to channels that will not interfere with each other in effect means that license holders have a fair guarantee of a profitable business. In exchange, television stations are expected to act to an arguable degree in accord with the conception of the public interest held by the FCC and Congress, whether or not doing so maximizes profits.

Despite these circumstances, American television by the standards of much of the world is thoroughly nonpaternalistic. Public broadcasting, like commercial broadcasting, exists because of the licenses made available by the FCC. However, it has not so far received the financial support to give it much weight in the totality of television viewing by the American people. In most areas on most evenings, public television attracts less than 5 percent of the audience viewing television, and an estimate that nationally 95 percent of what Americans watch daily on television is commercial programming would complement "public" television's lack of magnetism. In most countries, if there is a system of broadcasting dependent on advertising, it must compete with a strong system operating free of such support. Industrialized or not, Western, Soviet, Asian, Third World, or "other" in orientation or location—elsewhere we find broadcasting systems created to serve a programming philosophy. In some cases, these systems are government-run; in other instances, as with Great Britain's BBC (British Broadcasting Corporation), the system is independent of the government and insulated from its direct influence. These systems are supported by taxes, fees levied on television set owners, or both. The puny role in America of broadcasting independent of commerce is the exception, not the rule—although hardly by that fact discreditable.

This proportionately minuscule share of public television in the attention devoted to the medium by the public is the product of the meager and generally uncertain financial support allocated to such broadcasting. The framework, although certainly open to an expanded place for noncommercial public radio and television, was constructed in the first days of radio and made firm by the Communications Act of 1934. From the beginning, the priority was given to broadcasting conducted as a business, deriving its income from the sale of time to advertisers. Such time, the analogue of space in newspapers and magazines, naturally increases in value as the size and purchasing power of the audience increases. William J. McGill, president of Columbia University and chairman of the second Carnegie Commission on public broadcasting, was correct in remarking with the release of the commission's 1979 report, *The Public Trust,* that much of the fate and character of American broadcasting had been settled long ago. "We couldn't go back 50 years and change everything," he said, perhaps wistfully, in explaining the commission's argument for much stronger financing for new programming rather than the creation of a new national network or the shift of the many public stations from the difficult-to-receive UHF to the far superior VHF frequencies occupied by commercial broadcasters.

What happened, simply, is that the federal government aligned itself with the values of private enterprise in devising a system of broadcasting, and then in accord with the deep-rooted American distrust of those same values established a means to temper the outcome. There is a probably justified self-suspicion in the 1934 Act's prohibition against stipulating program content, yet the obligation to review the performance of broad-casters at regular intervals implies unambiguously a concern over content. The solution has been various requirements that presumably shape but do not mold content—the Fairness Doctrine, requiring equal treatment of controversial issues; the preference for local ownership, which ostensibly enhances the likelihood of public service; the policy that public service is incomplete without news; a hostility to monopolization of broadcast outlets or the varied media in a community, on the grounds that single ownership threatens the diversity of viewpoints to which the public has access; and the demand that the broadcasters by some means regularly study their communities to ascertain what the community thinks about the way the broadcaster conducts his business. What immediately and largely determines content, however, is the invisible hand of economics— and in this instance it has forever tied programming to popularity. In the American system of broadcasting, the first step was not a conviction about the effort programming should make to serve the country, but the adop-tion of a means by which any handwringing over such a conviction could be evaded. The decisions are made by what reaps a profit. That was true for radio; it became true for television.

This technological innovation—the country's primary medium of enter-tainment today, the scourge of Presidents, adored by children, and so successful that it is journalistic practice to wisecrack that a television station entails a license to print money—was first placed on display as a technological curiosity at public events in the United States in the latter half of the 1930s. Partly because of the delay in development caused by World War II, it remained an exotic novelty until the mid-1950s, when the television set gradually became a common item in American living rooms.

Today almost every household reports to the U.S. Bureau of the Census that its possessions include one or more television sets, and at least three-fourths of households have color sets. On any fall day in the late 1970s, the set in the average television-owning household was on for about seven hours. Between 8 and 9 p.m. on a typical fall evening, the audience would be about half the country—100 million persons. Such extraordinary presentations as the Super Bowl (which transforms football from a team and league sport to a test of "the right stuff"), Alex Haley's *Roots,* and debates between presidential aspirants can attract 75-100 million viewers.

There are about 950 licensed television stations in operation. Somewhat more than 700 stations are managed as privately owned, profit-seeking ventures. These stations broadcast annually more than four million hours of programming. About 250 public and educational stations supported by contributions and subsidies add 1.4 million hours. Most homes, even in remote areas, have access to several stations, and an increasingly larger proportion—but far from a majority—can subscribe to cable or pay-TV services for additional programming.

The three giant national networks—the American Broadcasting Company, the Columbia Broadcasting Company, and the National Broadcasting Company—are the nervous system of American television. Just as American television is almost synonymous with commercial television, commercial television is almost synonymous with network television. About 90 percent of the privately owned stations are affiliated with one of the networks, and the networks provide about two-thirds of their programming. The rest of commercial programming—on nonaffiliated stations and in time not covered by the networks—is either locally produced or, far more frequently, purchased from independent producers and suppliers. Often the purchases are of programs originally disseminated by the networks, and the widespread reliance on reruns enlarges the network presence in American television.

The principal involvement of the government in commercial television has been through the FCC. This agency, authorized by the Communications Act of 1934, literally determines the structure of American television by setting the rules to which broadcasters have to conform. It allocates available spectrum space among uses (such as commercial versus public television); determines the privileges—until, in some instances, halted by the courts—that commercial "open air" broadcasters, cable, pay-TV, and other communications operators enjoy; and licenses television stations. In principle, the FCC could revoke a station license under periodic review, but in practice it has seldom done so, although license renewals have been challenged frequently by would-be broadcasters and dissatisfied citizen groups. It requires a "reasonable" amount of news and community-oriented programming, and as long as this vague criterion has not been scandalously violated the renewal of a license is not in jeopardy.

Both the language of the authorizing statute and the free speech guaranty of the First Amendment constrains the agency from interfering in programming. Many have argued that the FCC could exercise extensive influence over programming by increased scrutiny during license renewal. The premise is that the obligation to oversee the public interest conveys the power to reject the distribution of a broadcast schedule among categories of programming, but not the treatment or expression of views occurring within a category. The precise boundaries of its power in regard to programming can only be determined by court test—an event contingent on a disputed action.

Many would hold that the FCC has been at least as adept at the sidestep as the forward step. Barry Cole and Mal Oettinger chose *Reluctant Regulators* for their account of the FCC for precisely that reason. Cole is a professor who spent several years at the FCC; Oettinger has closely followed broadcast regulation as a journalist. They describe an agency made hesitant by lack of expertise, inadequate data, and continual and close association of its staff and commissioners with the businessmen on whose behavior they are supposed to pass judgment. Reluctance was enhanced by the frequency with which these officials find subsequent lucrative careers in some field of communications. Vincent Mosco, a sociologist who served as a fellow at the now-defunct White House Office of Telecommunications Policy, reinforces such a view in his analysis of the treatment of the four major broadcasting innovations of the television era: FM, UHF, cable, and pay-TV. In each case, he concludes that the FCC opted for the status quo and what had been demonstrated to be feasible—to the profit of the broadcasters in place and to the detriment of technological innovation.

There are several exceptions where the federal government has become involved in the content of what is broadcast. Two became the concern of the FCC because of provisions of the 1934 Act and its revision: (1) The Fairness Doctrine, requiring full and impartial treatment of controversy, and (2) the Equal Time law, requiring that candidates for public office be given equivalent opportunities for broadcast exposure. The first, which demands of broadcasters that they cover not only important public issues but all sides of issues as well, is the foundation for the obligation imposed on radio and television to provide news and public affairs programming. Its broadest interpretation occurred when, prior to being outlawed by Congress, cigarette commercials could be aired only if antismoking appeals also

were scheduled. A third involves the FTC. This agency has the responsibility to protect viewers from deception and misleading claims, and it is
because of such authority that the FTC initiated extended hearings in
1979 on the propriety and influence of advertising directed to children.

Children's programming illustrates the impotence that besets the FCC
in regard to broadcast content. The agency's 1974 policy statement
advanced a number of auspicious phrases as guidelines for broadcasters,
such as "diversified programming," programming that would "further the
educational and cultural development of the child," "age-specific" programming for preschool and school-age children, and more programming
during weekdays. Late in 1979 a special staff assigned to study children's
programming acknowledged that these admonitions had largely been ignored. In effect, it admitted that a policy statement that goes against
economic interest without including forceful means of implementation is
not policy, but wishful thinking. The staff proposed that a major option
open to the agency was to require a certain number of hours per week of
programming—specifically, it suggested that broadcasters be required to
present each weekday between 8 a.m. and 8 p.m. five hours of "educational or instructional programming" for preschool children and two and
one-half hours for school-age children. The power of the FCC to mandate
such action, as well as the wisdom of doing so, is certain to be challenged
by broadcasters, for their economic interest lies with entertainment programming drawing as wide an age spectrum as possible. Whatever the
outcome of this newly vigorous posture on the part of the FCC, it conveys
a tale of powerlessness as much as it does of potential authority. The staff
concedes that the FCC can do no more; whether such hours would be
filled with invention or bargain-basement pedagogy is anyone's guess. The
dependence on the marketplace simply proscribes effective reform. Thus,
the staff declaration rises to a note of humility—and urges Congress to do
more for children's television through public television and a National
Endowment for Children's Television.

Policy in regard to what will be broadcast as entertainment has always
been set by the broadcasters themselves. Policy, of course, is implicitly
made in the many and varied decisions that lie behind the production of a
particular program. The absence of a public, formal declaration of intent
beyond the acknowledged desire to attract as many viewers as possible
does not imply a lack of overall uniformity or coherence to what is
broadcast. It only means that policy emerges from the structure of
broadcasting rather than being imposed by those who rule it—and here
programming strategies and judgments about what will appeal to the
audience, as exemplified in the manufacture of situation comedies in the
latter half of the 1970s to win over young viewers who often play a large

role in selecting what a family views during primetime, will approximate a formal policy.

Policy is explicitly made in the formulation and enforcement of codes to which broadcasters declare their allegiance. The function of these self-regulatory codes is to protect broadcasting from governmental attempts at intervention and harassment by politicians and the public. Like all mass media, television is asymmetrical in respect to approval and approbation. Approval is largely influential only when in the form of popularity, which in the case of television means ratings (the proportion of the possible audience viewing) and shares (the proportion of those viewing who are tuned to a particular program). Praise from the prominent or ardent applause from some small segment of the audience are welcome, but do not typically become strictures for future programming. Offending any part of the audience, however, is generally avoided except when offense to a few may seem the price of popularity, for outrage involves the broadcaster in a conflict when he would prefer to do business. Broadcasting codes are designed to minimize such conflict by symbolizing pure motives, minimizing actual offense, and precluding material that might somehow harm someone either directly or indirectly through the encouragement of violent or destructive behavior.

The most publicized of these shields is the Television Code of the National Association of Broadcasters (NAB), to which the three networks and many stations subscribe, although each network and some stations also have their own codes. Such codes set standards in regard to violence, sexual relations, obscenity, the occult, advertising, and other content. However, because the NAB imposes no sanctions beyond the denial of an offender's right to display the NAB seal, the code is little more than a symbol. That symbol is very important to broadcasters in convincing Congress and the public that they behave conscionably, and documented violation is an embarrassment. Widespread or extensive violation would readily become the basis for demands for regulatory experimentation. Self-regulation everywhere in business is the first defense against intervention by statute or government agency. The NAB code may be bereft of sanctions, but not of influence.

In theory, the responsibility for what is broadcast rests with the individual station. The courts have made it clear that responsibility is not only legally vested in the broadcaster but that he cannot assign it to anyone else. For example, in the "family viewing" litigation, the federal court in Los Angeles ruled in 1976 that subscription to the NAB or any other code could not be required of broadcasters as a condition of membership or any other privilege. "Family viewing" involved the near-universal accession of the major entities in broadcasting—the networks and the NAB—to a restriction between 7 and 9 p.m. on violence and sexually provocative programming ostensibly unsuited for young viewers. This more stringent code had the lifespan of a housefly. Initiated the year before at the urging of then-FCC Chairman Richard Wiley who was attempting to placate a restive Congress, it was immediately challenged by the Hollywood writers and producers. Their forward flag was the First Amendment. At the flank was formal FCC action, with its procedural safeguards of hearings and votes. Both, the plaintiffs said, had been violated by the role taken by the chairman, who personally argued for compliance by telephone call, letter, and meeting; his position, they alleged, implied official intervention. The banner they grasped most firmly, however, was probably the claim of financial injury, for the new restriction in effect reduced the hours for which past and present programming judged to violate the code could be marketed. Judge Warren Ferguson concurred with the plaintiffs—and in his ruling struck at the notion that standards from any source could be imposed in any way on the individual broadcaster. This foray into ex officio policy-making is now subject to the destiny of judicial appeal, and in one guise or another will probably again become a problem for the FCC—which could attempt to proceed in the same direction formally—and eventually a matter for adjudication by the U.S. Supreme Court.

The most amusing aspect of the venture were the forces arrayed in opposition. Action for Children's Television (ACT) chose to oppose family viewing as a code provision, because it feared that such a measure would provide the broadcasters with a public justification for not immediately undertaking further reforms. The NAB and the three networks which had agreed to adopt the code were not only joined with the FCC and Chairman Wiley as defendants, but the NAB and two of the networks remained with the FCC and Chairman Wiley as appellants in seeking to have a First Amendment verdict in their behalf reversed. There were, of course, the possible damages stemming from the brief period in which the code restricted the marketplace for television programs, but there was also a motive converse to that of ACT—for the broadcasters anxiously desire a visible code that they can point to as exemplifying effective self-regulation, for protection against critics.

In practice, code enforcement falls to the three networks. Individual broadcasters typically have neither the time, interest, nor sufficient advance opportunity to rule on content. Each of the networks maintain broadcast standards departments that function as censors by applying their interpretations of the NAB and the network's own code to new programming. At each stage in the production process, from initial concept to final cut, they rule on acceptability. What reaches the screen is shaped by them and sometimes is the result of protracted negotiations among the broadcast standards departments, the programming departments that select each season's offerings, and the production companies. Because much of what is broadcast are reruns of earlier network programming, this department's influence extends far beyond the current network schedules.

The federal government is a major financial contributor to public broadcasting, but its influence over American programming officially has been largely limited to enforcement of the Fairness Doctrine and the equal time law. Public television, like commercial, has a national distribution system, but unlike commercial television there are no networks supplying an extensive schedule that stations will broadcast concurrently. Time not consumed by the nationally distributed programming, as in commercial television, is filled by local production and acquisitions. The principal exception to federal involvement has been direct support for a few programs aimed at specific audiences, such as parents and ethnic minorities, and here the government's role stops at making such programs available.

The advantage of the American system is, of course, the minimization of the use of television by the government for its own purposes. In the United States, there is no voice of authority to cajole, threaten, or mislead over the airwaves. That an opportunity to do so is tempting to anyone in power, and particularly anyone threatened by the public, events, or foes, is demonstrated by the attempts—revealed only years later when documents became available to the press under the Freedom of Information Act—by the Nixon administration to reshape the journalism of public television. Here we find the perils of paternalism dramatized—the principal television reporter, Sander Vanocur, was to be discredited by planted stories about his "excessive" salary; the power of local outlets, thought to be more conservative than the national Corporation for Public Broadcasting, was to be increased over selection of all programming; and the governing board at the national level was to be packed with persons ideologically aligned with the administration. The 1979 report of the Carnegie Commission on the Future of Public Broadcasting responds to this danger by advancing numerous proposals for increasing the insulation from government of public television. What the report also makes clear is that the American system is unusual in its reliance on business success:

> The United States is the only Western nation relying so exclusively upon advertising effectiveness as the gatekeeper of its broadcasting activities. The consequences of using the public spectrum primarily for commercial purposes are numerous, and increasingly disturbing. The idea of broadcasting as a force in the public interest, a display case for the best of America's creative arts, a forum of public debate—advancing the democratic conversation and enhancing the public imagination—has receded before the inexorable force of audience maximization [McGill, 1978].

ENTERTAINMENT

The consequence of the means by which nonpaternalism has been achieved is the unabashed emphasis of television on entertainment. The arbiter of commercial broadcasting—and because it is so dominant, of American television itself—is competition for the audience. It is audience size and character that determines the profit for the broadcaster. Popularity is the goal, with size modulated in importance by the desire to attract viewers in the 18 to 55 age bracket that constitutes the principal market for consumer goods. Popularity does not simply rule entertainment—it makes entertainment the principal dimension of commercial television.

When the schedule of a typical public television station is compared with that of a commercial station, one of the more striking contrasts is the greater proportion of the public schedule devoted to news and informational programming. About 15 percent of the total broadcast minutes of network television are devoted to news and public affairs. Because news programming attracts a smaller proportion of the viewing public than does evening entertainment, and because much public affairs programming is scheduled in periods of low viewing, such as on Sunday morning, their actual share in the television consumed by the public is even more modest. When the trend over the years in public television is examined, there appears to be an increase in the proportion of the schedule devoted to entertainment. This tendency for public to follow commercial television is the result of public television's susceptibility to the idolatry of popularity. *Of course* the entertainment purveyed by public television is typically different from that offered by the networks; who would argue otherwise? *Of course* network television often offers programming risky in audience appeal and as adventuresome, serious, and cultural as anything attempted by public television; no sensible person would say differently. The point is that entertainment is surer than information to attract an audience, and thus the dominance of entertainment in American television is inevitable.

Entertainment as a concept has the encompassing reach of the 1940s comic book hero, Plastic Man. Without painful stretching, it will include literature, poetry, music, and *The Gong Show*. Although entertainment occurs whenever we are not entirely motivated, in attending to something, by a desire for information or by the benefits of study, neither this nor any other feature these varied ways of spending time have in common bestow equal merit to the consumer, the producer, and the product. Entertainment embraces what should be called trash as well as that to which only fools would deny the label of art. The fact that there is often disagreement about precise ranking does not invalidate belief in a hierarchy of worth based on something other than popularity, or make less ludicrous the idea that public attention implies any value other than itself.

The significant feature of television entertainment is not that it shares qualities with other entertainment, but that it serves primarily as a vehicle for advertisers. Should a broadcaster be so rude as to dream himself Picasso, he would find his concern for his programs about as deep as the painter's for his canvas—an important element, surely, but hardly the essence of the matter. Even being popular is not enough, as it might be for a novel or a play, for the pitting of program against program in the same time slot leaves no ambiguity about superiority, and superiority by the criterion of the largest potential market for the goods to be hawked is what will bring the greatest revenue from advertisers. Broadcasters, hardly fools, would certainly acknowledge that what is good for advertisers may not be good for the public, but by their actions they rate the good of television and advertisers alike if not identical.

Erik Barnouw, the Columbia University professor acknowledged to be the leading historian of broadcasting, recounts many tales of how advertisers have gone beyond mere appeal in shaping programs to their ends. Sponsorship by cigarette makers meant that there could be no smoking by villains, coughing by anyone, or fires anywhere—for all might reflect unfavorably on the product. Similar protection has been extended to other products. Controversy, of course inevitable to some degree, was so avoided that one drama of racial prejudice was rewritten into a story of hostility toward a new neighbor without apparent explanation—until at the very end it is revealed he is an ex-convict. Blacklisting during the McCarthy Era became for sponsors simply a sensible means of not risking offense, and thus they became conspirators in the denial on the basis of political affiliation, rumor, and innuendo of the opportunity to work in or appear on television.

Barnouw suggests that drama that has emotional truth, a realism quite distinct from the accuracy of police procedure or the techniques of thieves, is incompatible with television because by contrast it emphasizes the triviality of commercials. He further argues that the very themes and substance of television entertainment derive from the needs of U.S. industry—from the game shows honoring lust for appliances to the action and adventure series that portray a world of threat and response not dissimilar to the way international corporations perceive the foreign relations of the United States.

The hegemony, or, in the case of the implicit message of entertainment, the calculation, of the hand applied to programming by the advertiser may be disputed, but not its continual presence—however deft and clandestine. The quiz shows of the late 1950s exemplify that hand at work. Several primetime programs gained great popularity by pitting contestants against each other for huge prizes—as the names of two, *The $64,000 Question* and *The $64,000 Challenge*, made clear. Then Herbert Stempel, a deposed

contestant, confirmed rumors that the contests were fixed to ensure
suspense and audience-pleasing participants. Investigations by a New York
grand jury and a congressional committee followed. Charles Van Doren, a
Columbia English instructor who won $129,000 and in so doing became a
highly paid television personality, confessed he had been fed answers in
advance. Behind the manipulations was the desire of the sponsor for a hit
show; as Van Doren told the committee, dishonesty was argued to be
permissible because it was "only entertainment." As the result of the
scandal, the networks began to take a larger role in programming rather
than leaving everything to the advertising agencies and the sponsors.
Today, series are no longer manufactured to the specification of a single
sponsor, and commercial time is sold for inclusion in programming produced to the expressed demands of the networks. Yet what the quiz shows
represented is no relic, for at their root was the organization of broadcasting around the principle of maximum popularity.

COMPETITION

Television in America is a business of unabashed competition. So, one
might remark, are all businesses. Competition in television differs, however, because of the gladiatorial aspect imposed by the character of the
medium and the way it is organized. The consequence is a drive on the
part of each of the three networks and of the stations within a market to
be first in the value to advertisers of the audiences assembled for their
programs.

As Les Brown, the New York *Times* television reporter, emphasizes so
astutely in his account of one season's struggle among the networks for
dominance in the ratings, television only appears to be in the business of
entertainment and news. In fact, it is in the business of vending the
attention of the public to parties interested in selling their products to that
public. Size of audience, modified somewhat by its predilection for consumption, is the determinant of profits.

Economists bicker over whether the proper criterion for assessing the
rate of return to broadcasters is capital investment, a standard by which
broadcasting becomes one of the most lucrative businesses in the United
States, or regular investment in new programming, by which it simply
becomes a very healthy business. However, there is no doubt that over the
years the three networks and most of the many hundreds of stations have
amply enriched their operators. To be "numero uno" in the ratings means
tremendous returns to a network. For example, when ABC in 1977 for the
first time became the profit leader, it reported an increase in one year of
almost 100 percent, rising from $83 million to $165 million in profits
before federal income taxes. In recent years, even to be third among the

networks in ratings has assured a substantial profit; but the system gives comfort only to being first, for there are not only the demands of the network organization itself—where jobs and salaries are dependent on financial success—and of the stockholders—who, like stockholders everywhere, want increased dividends and rising share values—but of the affiliate stations whose profits derive to a large extent from the success of network programming in attracting audiences.

Television is a mass medium that can enter at any moment almost every home in the country. Because of the continuing and pervasive measurement of audience size by the A.C. Nielsen Company and the Arbitron rating service of the American Research Bureau, the division of spoils at any given hour is seldom in doubt. The untended set, the inaccurate diary, the straying of viewers' attention to other activities—these anomalies may nurture the carpings of journalists about the accuracy of audience figures, but the measures undeniably provide a reliable currency for comparing performance. The dependence of profits on audience means that for any one competitor—station or network—it is always more desirable to attract as large a body of potential consumers as possible, thereby maximizing the price that advertisers will pay for access to them, than it is to expand the total audience in any given hour by offering something appealing to a smaller audience composed of individuals who would not ordinarily watch television. The strategy dictated by the system is widely popular fare that divides the audience for mass entertainment, not adventuresome programming.

Competition in television means a struggle each hour for dominance. The incentives discourage diversity, for a network audience of 10 million is not as valuable as an audience of 20 or 30 million, even if that 10 million were made up of viewers who otherwise might turn to something other than television. The capability of the medium to reach almost everyone, and the fusing of profits to appeal, leads to programming that across outlets tends to be much the same. Television operates like a game in which each player's return takes precedence over the total return to all players, and there is an inevitable narrowing and homogenization of what is offered coupled with the frequent head-to-head scheduling of the medium's starships of greatest interest. It ignores millions, yet squanders its best.

The 1970s will be recorded as the decade in which competition escalated from hard-fought to frenzied. The upward rush of ABC on a calculated appeal to the teenagers given control of the set by blasé adults ended a ratings hierarchy that had seemed to have the permanence of the pyramids. The third network, now first, had established strength in sports dazzlement before riding situation comedy to primetime preeminence. Later, it would turn to news as a still stationary front. Whether by chance or combustion, warfare became a good metaphor for what was taking place. The increasing production of made-for-TV movies, the emergence of miniseries, and the everhandy "special" made showboating a common term in television and something desperate always done by the other guy. Series were turned over as fast as cards at blackjack. The season for which programming was scheduled, once stretching from fall to spring, became two, then dissolved into hasty replacements and rearrangements. The success of such phenomena as *Roots* encouraged maneuvering, yet the breakup of stable schedules may have reduced habitual viewing. Second chances for series became as rare as second acts in American lives were thought to be by F. Scott Fitzgerald. Many wondered if an *All in the Family*, which took more than a season to build an audience, could survive in the new atmosphere.

The atmosphere exacerbated the dissension between network broadcasters and the Hollywood "hyphenates"—so-called because their jobs so frequently combine some portion of being a producer-director-writer—over the quality of programming. The Hollywood community, already beset by restrictions on violence, fiercely deplored the confinement of serious drama to luxury display, such as in *Holocaust*. The broadcasters spoke of business as usual. Yet it would be a mistake to think of the 1970s as only continuity, unless one is of the mind that nuclear war is on the same continuum as the spear. Conversely, it would be a mistake to think of conflict between the network and the Hollywood people as peculiar to the new rapacity.

The 1970s were new in the intensity of competition, but the values and interests of those who broadcast and those who create what is broadcast have never been in perfect congruence. The broadcasters are businessmen in the end even if they do not begin that way; anything else, given the way television is organized in America, would be gratuitous schizophrenia. The Hollywood people, however, bring to their jobs a residue of literary and journalistic intentions that have nothing to do with profits. They would like a system that provides opportunities to exercise originality, social concern—in short, a chance to parade themselves in the manner of poets or novelists. Whether rightly or wrongly, they believe that such opportunities have declined sharply over the past years. Of course, television does not encourage poor or clumsy work; the point at which these camps divide is whether what it does encourage is respectable, however skillfully executed. By the end of the 1970s, the Hollywood community, although turning out the shows as steadily as ever, was bitterly saying no.

News is no less subject to adversarial strategies as is entertainment. News programs must compete like other programming for a share of the audience, and news formats and news personalities become defunct with the absence of sufficient popularity. Entertainment programs begin a lengthy journey from concept to final cut many months before broadcast. En route, they are revised in accord with intuition, social policy directed against violence or in behalf of more prominent treatment of minorities or women, and research on their appeal. News formats undergo a similar honing. Reporters and anchormen are picked to attract viewers not fully enamored of the competition—so as one network or station finds a place in the minds and time budgets of viewers, the others will reshape their presentations by juggling age, sex, demeanor, and set decor to find a sentiment uncaptured. Public television, ostensibly removed from the fray, could no more escape fully from the pervading values than a school-child can evade George Washington's cherry tree. Audience attraction has become accepted as the measure of the medium, and public television must justify its governmental and private funding by demonstrating that it serves a need economically feasible to be met by and compatible with television. If a mass appeal is in conflict with many of its proffered goals, a negligible appeal is inconsistent with survival. Although the people who run public television often will explain to a critic that it is not intended to be popular, in fact it strains constantly, in accord with the urgings of critics and friends alike, to attract more and more viewers. Thus we find public television's trend toward entertainment over the years. It is only being true to its medium.

Except for the rare program put on by a local station, commercial programming is produced by organizations independent in ownership of the networks. This separation, although clouded by a history of network control and involvement in the honored proclivity of healthy firms to consume their suppliers, is the result of the application of the federal antitrust statutes to broadcasting. Ownership by the networks (three in number) of production companies was construed to infringe on competition, for what sensible oligopolist would buy from other than his own company? In practice, however, the networks determine what will be produced because they are the principal market for the goods in question. The antitrust action may have added vigor to business, but not necessarily to the home screen. The demands of the networks, canny if not always accurate in estimating popularity, not only influence first-run network-disseminated programming, but also the rest of programming—for nonnetwork television, whether from an independent station or during the open hours of an affiliate, consists to a considerable degree of reruns with the status and benefits of a second-hand car.

News and public affairs programming, unlike entertainment, are the products of the disseminators. Networks and stations make their own, with the former drawing somewhat on coverage either convertible by a turn of phrase or in fact a significant national story that their affiliates can provide. The daily selection and treatment of events are the responsibility of the news staff. These decisions are made autonomously of management. Yet news cannot escape the values of management, which reside in popularity. Journalists may manufacture the news, but management manufactures the newsmen and their tools. Formats and personnel are the creatures of management, as is the budget to do the job. Thus, news, like entertainment, becomes honed to exigencies of competition.

Marshall McLuhan designated television as a "cool" medium. He was right to argue that media have characteristics that impose some meaning of their own on what is conveyed and possibly apt in his metaphor; he could not have found a less accurate term for the way it transacts business.

THE FUTURE

The three terms—nonpaternalism, entertainment, and competition—will continue to describe American television despite the many changes certain to occur. Any recasting of the Federal Communications Act will change the way broadcasting does business in the 1980s and beyond, but not the pattern of broadcasting. The basic principle of obligation in exchange for privilege will survive; regulation, whatever the precise form, will continue as a gently applied hand; and the marketplace, defined much as it is today, will continue to dictate the content of television. The trend is toward a loosening of federal stipulations, not the abandonment of the system.

Even if the Carnegie Commission's proposals were resolutely followed, there would be no change in the preeminence of television designed to serve the needs of advertisers. The increasing of federal financial support for public broadcasting, the production of new programs on the basis only of expert advice about their cultural desirability, and the insulation of decision-making from federal influence will dress up the public television schedule, expand the audience, and offer programs that generally would not survive the gauntlet of commercial television—but they will not bring about a revolution in taste or business conduct. After a three- or even fourfold increase in the public television audience, television viewing by the public would remain almost 90 percent the products of commerce.

The principal source of change will be neither an altered federal posture nor the blooming of public television, but the technological developments that are changing the communications environment. There will always be television available free to viewers because of the revenue derived from the sale of advertising; networks will continue, for national programming will remain popular enough, despite inevitable declines in audience, to serve as vehicles for advertising. Nevertheless, there is a shift toward greater choice that is quantitatively large enough to suggest the beginning of an upheaval in mass media not unlike that which followed the introduction of television. The increasing availability of cable television with its many channels; the use of satellites to relay signals, which makes it possible for a so-called "super station" such as WTCG in Atlanta to reach, by feeding cable systems, more than 5 million homes across the country, thereby creating a distribution system for programming that competes with the networks; pay TV, an apparent financial success in its few trials; and video cassettes, video discs, and in-home playback and recording systems—these innovations mean that the seeker of entertainment and information will no longer be confined by the behavior of network and local broadcasters. With many consumers ascended to a throne of broader alternatives, new means to supply them will be encouraged, and conceivably television will come to more closely approximate book and magazine publishing in satisfying a variety of tastes and nurturing interests found only among a few. Even so, the step from technological capability to actuality is a long one. We would be quite mad to think that the new technology means the end of television as we have known it, and madder still to believe that television's impact will be lessened by innovations that will make the tube more appealing.

2

TIME AND TIME AGAIN

There is no more clearly documented way in which television
has altered American life than in the expenditure of time. It
has not only changed the way the hours of the day are spent,
but the choices available for the disposal of those hours, and in
so doing has brought the age of the mass media to maturity.
Television relentlessly devours time as if movie theaters had
opened up to embrace the communities around them, and
much is never again the same.

WATCHING

For a few brief moments when television was a novelty, people thought
they would cluster around the set as if it contained living bands of tiny
jugglers. This did not come to be so. Rapt attention is not unknown, but
"television viewing" as measured in hours and minutes means something
quite different from the same measure of sitting in a theater.

In the early 1960s, an advertising researcher named Charles Allen
placed time-lapse movie cameras in 100 homes in Kansas and Oklahoma
and took about a million photos at the rate of four per second. About ten
years later, Robert Bechtel again continuously monitored people watching
television. This time, video cameras relayed their images to constantly
manned mobile units parked in the yards of 20 Kansas City families, and
cameras simultaneously recorded behavior in front of the screen and what
was on the screen.

Allen found that for about a fifth of the time, the set entertained an
empty room. For another fifth of the time, whoever was in the room was
not looking at the set. He reported that children "eat, drink, dress and
undress, play [and] fight . . . in front of the set," and that adults "eat,
drink, sleep, play, argue, fight, and occasionally make love . . ." Bechtel
observed similar divided attention, ranging from housework to reading and
dancing; some people mimicked what they saw.

Surveys in the United States and abroad that have asked people to recall what they did while watching television also make it clear that the metaphor of a theater in the home does not fit television. Most often it is housework of one kind or another—washing, ironing, cleaning, and cooking—that accompanies viewing, but there is also plenty of talking and eating.

The films of people in their living rooms not only documented that television often plays to an indifferent house, but that attention varies with what is shown. Bechtel found that commercials were ignored more than programs, and that attention wavered almost as much for sports and news. Eyes were on the screen most constantly for movies and suspense tales. This is what a sensible person would expect. Commercials, sports, and news are all episodic; it is not necessary to follow them closely to learn as much as one could want. Commercials, in addition, are often redundant with their last transmission. The fact that commercials have about the same appeal as news and sports suggests that the public indulges in self-deception in singling out their banality and self-interest, for people turn away from such programming only to the degree consistent with their format.

Television viewing is discontinous. It is frequently nonexclusive. It is often interrupted. It changes with the type of program. All these are encompassed in the figures so lucratively vended by the A.C. Nielsen Company.

VIEWING

The "novelty hypothesis" was soon proposed, and lingers on despite more than two decades of failure. People still say that television viewing will decline as the novelty wears off. History has proven otherwise. What few would have predicted occurred—television viewing, measured by hours of set use in the average household, has risen steadily.

At the beginning of the 1960s the figure was slightly less than six hours a day. By the end of the 1970s, it was about seven hours. These are fall and winter figures; summer viewing is about 15 percent lighter. This upward trend has been accompanied by the convergence of differences in viewing based on social status and education. Over the years, television has grasped the public to its bosom ever tighter.

Television viewing always has been greater among those lower in socioeconomic status, with education making a greater difference than income. Education means many things, including more imagination in disposing of time and greater capacity to exercise that imagination. The term "book culture" was employed by the sociologist Rolf Meyersohn to describe the cultural allegiance of the better-educated which left them less interested in television. By the end of the 1970s, these socioeconomic differences appeared to be disappearing as the time available for viewing began to be exhausted among the less educated and the more educated became less hostile toward the medium.

Probably no small role has been played in this convergence of taste by the entry of the first television generation and those succeeding into the legion of college-educated. These are adults for whom television held none of the ominous qualities that it did for some of their parents. At the same time, we should not think of the greater acceptance of television by those with lower education as reflecting a lack of leisure opportunities. Television meant participation in American life, although of a new kind, and viewing among the less educated was greater, not lesser, for those with more hobbies and interests. It was not simply greater leisure opportunities that set the better educated apart, but leisure of a particular character—"book culture."

The remarkable aspect of viewing is how much alike everyone is. When in 1970 set use was 6.8 hours a day in households whose head had less than one year of college, it was 5.6 hours a day in those headed by someone with more years of schooling. In earlier and later years, the difference between these two groups never exceeds 45 minutes. Yet even this 1.2 hours, substantial as it is both absolutely and as a proportion, does not constitute two different worlds, but varying degrees of a common experience. And, as we shall see, what people choose to view is much more alike than one would guess from differences in their backgrounds and what they think and say about television.

There are other relationships between demographic characteristics and viewing. Women view more than men because of their captive proximity as housewives to a television set. As a group, persons over 55 or 65 view more than younger adults because of the greater free time of retirement—yet women will continue on the average to view more hours per day than older men because of their somewhat fewer outside contacts and obligations.

Blacks as a group would be expected to view more because of the larger proportion of households low in income and education. They do view more, but socioeconomic status falls short as an explanation. In this case, a very rare thing occurs. Ethnic background, and not the differences in income and education related to it, are at work; ironically so with a medium known for its ability to override distinctions within the audience and which gave almost no place to minorities for much of its history. The facts are simple. Blacks on the average view television more than do whites when socioeconomic status is equivalent. Blacks not only are typically more favorable toward television, but the inverse relationship between education and attitudes favorable to the medium does not characterize blacks. Educated blacks tend to be as favorable as or more favorable than those less educated. Blacks have also shifted toward using television as a major source of political information more rapidly than have whites.

What seems to be involved is a complete set of factors. As a new, national medium, television, despite largely ignoring minorities, did not inherit the same hostility blacks held toward other general audience media, particularly newspapers and magazines. Television also arrived just in time to give prominent coverage to the civil rights movement. Thus, the medium capitalized on trends in attitudes and history. At the same time, blacks generally were less imbued with the "book culture" promoted among whites by education; years of education simply did not quite mean the same thing for blacks as for whites in this particular respect. Blacks, because of integration, also would have been particularly curious about the white society portrayed on television. Finally, many blacks, because of racial bias as well as economic deprivation, had delimited leisure alternatives. What this overall pattern illustrates is that the mass audience is not one group, but a coalition of distinctive groupings.

LEISURE

In the mid-1960s, the Hungarian sociologist Alexander Szalai conducted an extraordinary investigation of modern times for the United Nations Educational, Social, and Cultural Organization (UNESCO). He directed teams in 12 countries in western and eastern Europe and the western hemisphere, including the United States, in surveying how men and women in cities spent each day. The resulting data tell us about the weight of work, sleep, travel to the job, cooking and eating, child care, and the mass media in the expenditure of time.

These data, analyzed by Szalai and the American opinion researchers John Robinson and Philip Converse, reinforce many impressions about the place of television in American life. Among the 12 countries, which included France, East and West Germany, Belgium, Yugoslavia, Poland, Hungary, the Soviet Union, and Peru, Americans were the most likely to view some television during a day, and those who watched on the average viewed for more hours than viewers elsewhere. If Japan had been included, only the Japanese would have outranked Americans in devotion to television. In the United States, television was the third greatest consumer of time, behind only sleep and work. These were the top three out of 37 activities exclusive of each other that people described as their primary activity at any given time. Television accounted for a full third of all leisure time, and about 40 percent of leisure when viewing described as secondary to some other activity, such as eating, was included. Television was first among leisure activity. Even socializing of all kinds, including conversations at home and away, did not challenge television's domination of free time; it accounted for only about a fourth of leisure. Reading, study, and other use of mass media accounted for only about 15 percent. Going somewhere and doing something—a hike, hunting, the opera, the Dallas Cowboys—made up only about five percent of leisure. Television had become the principal component of voluntary life in America.

The UNESCO data also crudely approximate the results of a gigantic experiment, for in many societies television saturation was incomplete and television set owners could be compared with nonowners. The groups otherwise were much alike, and the fact that comparisons could be made across several societies, as if a single experiment were replicated again and again, adds confidence that the results are not happenstance. A major effect of television appeared to be reduced sleep. Set owners in these various societies on the average recorded 13 minutes less of sleep per night. They also reported spending less time socializing away from home, listening to the radio, reading books, conversing, at the movies, on religion, in miscellaneous leisure and travel in behalf of leisure, and on household tasks. Dust mice proliferated; other media suffered.

There was also a marked *increase* in one kind of activity—total time each day devoted to the mass media, which increased by about an hour. Many other media suffered because of television, but the fascination of television itself was enough not merely to compensate for the time drawn from other media, but to move the mass media to a far more central position on the social stage.

MASS MEDIA

The stunning rise of television turned public life newly and sharply toward the mass media. The UNESCO studies estimate that television increased daily attention to the mass media by one full hour. Newspapers, magazines, books, radio—Gutenberg began *his* revolution in the fifteenth century, and Marconi started his at the beginning of the twentieth, but it was with the diffusion of television in mid-century, 500 years after the invention of cast metal type, that the mass media became an occupying invader of everyday life.

Television shrank, destroyed, or changed other media, so that the larger role for the mass media was in fact command seized by television. That new hour spent on the media was television viewing. Given the nature of television, this meant more entertainment, more stories and images acceptable to people all over the country with all sorts of backgrounds, and more attention by people to words and pictures and the symbols they constitute that were the same for everybody.

The mass media in the United States will never be what they were before television. Radio once not only held listeners for many more hours a day, but it was a medium resembling television. Huge, heterogeneous audiences tuned to comedy, drama, variety, music, and news programming disseminated by three major networks. Bob Hope is still known, but the big stars of those days are fading to nostalgia—*The Great Gildersleeve, Amos 'n'Andy,* Jack Benny. Radio became a largely local medium with each station aiming at a relatively homogeneous segment of the audience. Appeal is precise—Top 40, progressive rock, jazz, talk, news, foreign language. Cynics found it for the most part a vendor of music, operating as an adjunct of the record industry. In a big market, such as Los Angeles, there was even room for a station dedicated to the music of the big bands, surviving and defunct. By adding pictures to words, television replaced radio as the national medium of daily entertainment.

Movies changed, too. The UNESCO studies found that television set owners spent less time at the movies. The motion picture industry found that this was indeed true. By 1970, annual movie attendance was about 19 million, compared with 41 million 10 years earlier and 82 million in 1946. Closed theaters adorned every business district. Movie attendance was declining before television as people turned to activities—such as spectator sports and driving—suspended by World War II, yet television made certain there would be no reversal of the trend. At first, television was a dumping ground for movies that had exhausted their theater audience, but by the 1970s television had become a major source of income for moviemakers through primetime screenings of features and made-for-TV films.

Television also helped refashion the American film. By becoming the center of family entertainment, television reduced to insignificance one of the big movie audiences. Yet by being a home medium, television was restricted in what it dared to show. In the competition between the two media, movies became increasingly more violent and sexually provocative as they sought an audience of teenagers and adults. Television hurried in their wake. Violence became a staple of programming. Sexual provocation became progressively more frequent and explicit. The media took advantage of increasingly liberal public standards, but they also contributed to this permissiveness by what they displayed in their struggle.

The magazine business was transformed. At the end of the 1970s, several long-dead giants of earlier decades—*Life, Look,* and the *Saturday Evening Post*—were resurrected, but their editorial ambitions were hesitant and their readerships small compared with pretelevision days. Television, as did these magazines, appeals to a broad range of tastes—the mass audience heterogeneous in makeup. Television reduced the time available for magazine reading and undermined the magazines aiming at a mass audience by taking away advertising revenue. The multicolor full-page spread intended to sell America became the TV commercial. The demise of these magazines made available pocket change and time among consumers.

Magazines appealing in depth to narrower tastes—*Gourmet, Yachting, Road and Track, Playboy*—prospered as readers and advertisers converged on the sharp focus not congenial to television.

Comic books surrendered many of the action- and humor-seeking young readers to television. Sales were 600 million in 1950; by 1970 they were half that. Television supplied the same kind of excitement in a cheaper, more convenient, and possibly more entrancing manner.

One might expect book publishing to be largely unaffected by television. One must guess again—and it was not only a matter of television consuming time that might be spent reading. Very early it became apparent that television, a medium immersed in popular fantasy, was depressing the library circulation of fiction without having a similar effect on nonfiction. Television did not supply the information of nonfiction, but substituted for some of the dreams of fiction. Publishing reflected this in the decline of titles of works of the imagination—fiction, poetry, and drama—from 22 to 13 percent of trade books between 1950 and 1970. Publishers also began to think of television as a means of promotion for books and to select titles for suitability as the topics of talk shows. The novel that becomes famously popular is an ideal servant of two masters, giving the publisher access to television and television something to talk about. Hermann Hesse would not have found a seat saved. Equally suited to the medium are books about the body, the mind, possessions, and money. They exploit self-interest and anxiety, and labeled as factual, they give the unimaginative assurance that there is some truth inside. The celebration of fame and passage to an inner circle of personal and material privilege became two preoccupations of television. The narcissism that seemed to pervade life in the second half of the century and celebrated by such phrases as the "me generation," the "politics of mellow," and "self actualization" was partly packaged by television's literary sideline.

Newspapers at first sometimes refused to print TV schedules in fear of aiding a competitor. They soon learned that television was something else people wanted to read about as well as watch. Leo Bogart, an extremely careful analyst of trends in media popularity, concluded after two decades of television that daily newspaper circulation had not been adversely affected. Time spent reading newspapers probably declined; big-city dailies folded one after another as people moved to the suburbs after World War II and labor and distribution costs rose. However, circulation increased evenly with population growth, for local newspapers could provide information through news and advertising unsuited to the brevity of television news and television commercials. Readership, in the sense of amount of attention, declined, but not in terms of audience size.

Newspapers and certain kinds of books are not the sole examples that television was not in all ways subtractive. Television adversely affected some

activities as it did some media, but it also drew attention to and enshrined
others. The entertainment nightly at home and the coverage of glamorous
sports events turned the minor league diamonds ghostly, with attendance
falling from 42 million in 1949 to 10 million 20 years later. Other sports
gained. Professional football became so popular that Congress was called
upon to mandate the televising of games once a sell-out was assured, and
television created a new national holiday in Super Bowl. For one day each
year, the entire nation focuses on a few panting men on a playing field.
Tennis and golf enlarged their publics. An occasional horse, such as Seattle
Slew, Affirmed and Alydar, and Spectacular Bid, became known to school-
children and millions of others totally unfamiliar with the magnetism of
the pari-mutuel machine.

Nevertheless, television and its technological evolution poses a continuing threat to other activities dependent on disposable time and income. Per capita daily newspaper circulation has not so far markedly
declined, but there are many reasons for fear and trembling among their
publishers. Not only has per capita circulation not increased over the
years, as one might expect with rising levels of education and proportion
of persons with college degrees, but the time available to peruse the
newspaper has been further reduced, reducing somewhat more the value to
an advertiser of newspaper space. Furthermore, the mid-1970s saw signs of
what might be the beginning of a downturn in per capita circulation.

Any further increases in television set use attributable to the greater
variety of offerings made available by cable, pay-TV, and in-home recording and playback will impose a further curtailment on time, and the
greater ability of cable to reach small, selected audiences in behalf of local
advertisers may undercut the revenues on which newspapers depend. Book
publishers and book clubs may find the world one of scarcity in the
coming years if network television, as it is almost certain to do, increasingly offers made-for-television movies exploiting the public's apparently
enormous appetite for venal glamor satisfied by pop novels about life at
the top and if cable and pay-TV package the same vicarious excitation in
exchange for fees that formerly were available for book buying.

Television, by directing attention, became an arbiter of the success of
others. When television drew attention to something far better than what
was at hand in real life, real life suffered. Live, minor league baseball could
not compete. When it drew attention to something of which people might
want more, real life benefited. In England, for example, television apparently markedly increased attendance for horse racing, horse jumping, and
major soccer confrontations by making these events newly important to
the public. The same thing occurs repeatedly not only with sports, but
with the rest of that five percent of leisure that is devoted to doing
something or going someplace—culture, live entertainment, the outdoors.

With sports, however, television established an uneasy symbiosis. It guaranteed some financial success by the fees paid for televising the event; conceivably it could be the architect of greater popularity, yet it also could destroy a sport by exhausting public interest. Colleges began to think of televised sports as synonymous with endowments and alumni gifts as sources of income. They, the promoters of professional sports, and the medium entered into a never-ending nervous dance.

Most people, if asked how television viewing affects their lives, would say that it seldom interferes with anything important. There is good reason to think they are wrong. Sleep, social interaction, and reading would be said to be unimportant by few, yet they have been reduced by television. Television has also severely altered the available options for the expenditure of time. Increasing set use implies more, not less, of both kinds of influence.

WHAT THE PUBLIC THINKS

Television occupies an ambiguous place in the American mind. It has increasingly gained more attention over the years, yet has fallen in public esteem. People watch more but like it less. Those who criticize it apparently often fail to act in accord with their words. Television holds its detractors in the same spell as its fans.

In 1960, Gary Steiner conducted a wide-ranging examination of public opinion about television, drawing on two-hour interviews with a representative national sample of about 2,400 adults and more in-depth study of a few hundred adults in a single city. Ten years later, Robert Bower did much the same thing.

As far as can be told from more recent studies, the trends and the pattern revealed by these two investigations continue to the present day. The portrait has many apparent contradictions; Could it be different for something that engages us so continually and so often?

The public by any absolute measure remains very favorable toward television. A sizable majority of the public will endorse television as valuable, interesting, exciting, worthwhile, informative, imaginative, and generally excellent. About half the public will say it is getting better. Nevertheless, there has been a definite decline in public satisfaction since 1960. Fewer people will endorse such statements today than two decades ago, and more believe that television is getting worse.

This shift is not as incongruous with the upward trend in hours of television consumed per day as it first appears to be. There is probably some tendency for the public to have stronger opinions, pro and con, about particular programs. Television's ubiquity may have encouraged a few to be more stringent in what they demand. More importantly, the increase in consumption represents changing norms about the acceptability of television viewing. Turning on the set, whatever the hour, has become more frequently the equivalent of switching on the lights. As the public with each passing year has increasingly accepted television as a constant glow in the household, it also has become more jaded about it.

The change in the status of the medium, from forefront to background, is exemplified by the motives the public declares for viewing. About the same proportions as in 1960 a decade later would declare that they viewed television to enjoy a favorite program, to see something said to be special, just to watch television, or to learn something. Far fewer designated television as "a pleasant way to spend an evening." Over the years, television has become less often the nightly focus of life and more a medium of passive acceptance.

The fluctuating ratings and the enormous audiences occasionally assembled for spectacular presentations would seem to belie the notion that many people simply watch television without much regard for what they are watching, but this is precisely what takes place. Broadcasters apply the phrase "least objectionable programming" to the most popular offering at any hour in recognition of this fact. Of course there is extensive selectivity as viewers attempt to find the most acceptable program once they are watching. The harsh competition among broadcasters would be justified even if only a small proportion of viewers could be diverted from one program to another, for a single point in the ratings represents several million viewers and a substantial difference in what advertisers can be charged. Nevertheless, a very sizable proportion of the audience at any given time on a typical evening watches a program because it appears on the channel to which the set is already tuned or because someone else in the household desires to watch the program. About three or four out of every 10 viewers admit to such daily seduction. The broadcasters exercise canniness, not indifference, in thinking about audience flow and the funneling of viewers from a popular program to subsequent offerings. Typically, television is consumed as a medium and the decision to view ordinarily takes precedence over the selection of what to view. Television is television first, programs second.

Despite its inclination to offer itself passively to television, the public places a positive value on its viewing. When asked to explain their viewing the night before, a large majority will advance reasons positive in tone, such as "to be entertained," "to be diverted," and "to relax." Very few will offer a derogatory phrase, such as "to kill time." Yet there is not much enthusiasm. In such querying of the public, about four out of five viewers will assert that they liked what they saw, but only about half as many will designate what they saw as "really worth watching." Nor, as the filming of viewers in their homes indicates, do they give close attention to what they view. About a fourth of those who say they watched a program will confess not following it from beginning to end, and about a third will be unable to give an accurate account the next day of what transpired.

However, despite the degree of passivity associated with viewing, the public discriminates not only enough to produce the well-known volatility in program popularity that makes American television what it is, but also reacts quite differently to the programs that it watches. Roderic Gorney, a Los Angeles psychiatrist, and his colleagues David Loye and Gary Steele assessed the psychological rewards that subscribers to a cable television system believed they received from programs they agreed to watch. They found that the extent to which programs were judged as satisfying or arousing in regard to intellectual, emotional, aesthetic, or moral reward varied greatly, as did the degree to which they were said to be arousing or satisfying as entertainment.

The widespread passivity also does not imply a homogeneous reaction to programming. Not only does amount of viewing differ by socioeconomic status, sex, age, and ethnicity, but the audience consists of various groupings distinguishable by somewhat different interests. Ronald Frank and Marshall Greenberg, two marketing researchers, analyzed the viewing behavior and the interests and characteristics of a sample of about 2,500 Americans 13 years of age and older. They found that it was possible to identify 14 non-overlapping miniaudiences, each of which varied from one another in age, income, basic interests, and television viewing. There is, for example, a component of the public oriented toward their families, largely made up of women who are white and have children, who are above average in the viewing of educational programs and programs with a broad appeal that allows them to use television as a means for family interaction and enjoyment. There is another component largely made up of young (average age, 29) blue-collar adults interested in noncompetitive activities such as fishing, camping, and auto repair who, because they are below average in the desire for involvement with others but above average in the desire for escape and creative accomplishment, are low in their viewing of talk shows and soap operas, but above average in their viewing of science fiction, adventure, action, and crime programs. Among the 14 miniaudiences, there are three predominantly of adult men, four predominantly of adult women, three representing young adults, one of male adolescents, two of female adolescents, and four evenly balanced between adult men and women. Thus, the great audiences that are assembled for some television programs in fact are analogous to the coalitions of groups with diverse and sometimes conflicting interests assembled by political leaders in national elections.

Better-educated viewers from the very first days of commercial television in the United States have been more critical toward the medium.

Favorable opinions, as well as viewing itself, have been inversely related to socioeconomic status. As television has become more firmly established as part of American life, the differences in viewing have become less pronounced. Attitudes have not so clearly converged. However, the in-depth studies of viewers in selected cities by Steiner and Bower have demonstrated that what better-educated viewers say is not clearly reflected in what they do. Better-educated viewers will declare that they want more informational programming and entertainment of greater seriousness and cultural quality, but when what they choose to view is matched against the choices of those with less education there is little discernible difference. Of course, education and other differences in background shape tastes and preferences in television programming, but the notion that better-educated viewers behave in a markedly different way toward their television sets is false. What is least objectionable to others is similarly least objectionable to them, and they divide their viewing between comedy, adventure, and public affairs programming about the same way as everybody else. They are somewhat more likely to watch public television, but as a group they are not particularly more selective in the rest of their viewing.

What people complain about most frequently are commercials and the entry into the home of material deemed unsuitable for children. When asked, about three-fourths of the public will endorse the view that there are too many commercials. Sizable proportions will agree that commercials are banal, annoying, misleading, "stupid," boring, or in poor taste. About half the public will agree that children "see things they shouldn't" on television, with a majority of these critics singling out violence, crime, and ostensibly frightening scenes. About one out of five fearful for children object to sexual suggestiveness, and a similar proportion think that questionable morals are advocated. About half the public accepts the hypothesis that portrayals of aggressive and criminal behavior may encourage young viewers to act likewise. Besides these objections based on content, there is also about a third of the public that believes television harms children by distracting them from more beneficial activities.

These objections are canceled as sources of widespread disaffection by attitudes held concurrently by the public. About three-fourths also subscribe to the view that commercials are a "fair price" for "free" entertainment, and support for the concept of advertising as a means of supporting entertainment has shown no signs of declining over the decades—although fully one-half, markedly more than in the past, think that television advertising is generally misleading. Those who oppose, for various reasons, the advertising directed at children on programming designed for them apparently have been successful in arousing public opinion, for about three-fourths of the public, when asked, now concur that advertising to children under eight years of age and the advertising of heavily sugared products to those under twelve should be banned or restricted. Further, a majority of respondents believes that commercials on such programming should be fewer in number than at present—but fewer than one out of five believes that commercials should be banned entirely from children's television. About three-fourths subscribe to the view that children are "better off" with than without television. Four out of five adults believe that television has educational advantages for children, with only about a fifth as many citing as an advantage the entertainment it provides or its function as a baby sitter. Such esteem extended in behalf of the young similarly shows no sign of declining with the passage of time.

The fact is that the public is satisfied with television much as it is. It will endorse various complaints, but it will also endorse views that imply reform is unnecessary. People are inarticulate and unsure of what they want from entertainment until they experience something of which they can say they want more. Works of the imagination are produced by the few because the capability is not present in the many. The public does not place television in any respect high on its agenda of concern. War, unemployment, crime, energy, personal comfort, and their many permutations occupy the public, not the media. The quality of vicarious experience may be paramount to those who create it, but not to its consumers. That the public will nod approval to criticisms of television means that sporadically the few who do care can marshal popular opinion, but the conflicting sentiments and indifference of the public also means that such opinion has no lasting force.

3

NEWS AS DIVERSION

News is governed by events. It is also governed by those who manufacture the "news." News is limited by what happens, but what eventually is packaged for public consumption becomes justified by the label applied to it. Human judgment and caprice, as well as the events themselves, enter in. This is not more true of television news than news in other media. What makes television news distinct are the numerous circumstances peculiar to the medium that order the decision-making of its journalists. They are many; news is made somewhat differently by each of the media.

THE SETTING

Television news, whether local or network, conforms to its medium and the economic and regulatory milieus in which that medium functions. Television is a visual medium, and "talking heads" are held in low repute by its practitioners. Television news gives priority to events amenable to film coverage—and film available is a large step toward inclusion in a newscast. It favors the dramatic and the exciting; nowhere do people so clearly figure in the news as on television. States of mind are not photogenic. In translating them into visual terms, the image takes over from the cerebral and what was construed as illustration becomes the essence of coverage. We get election campaigns as motorcades and crime as a young man talking into a microphone beneath the marquee of the sleazy motel thought to have housed a killer.

These aspects of television news would be mistakenly attributed if the cathode ray tube were held totally responsible. They represent the use of the medium for maximum appeal, and their roots are found in the hunger of those in the television business for popularity and profits. Television news emphasizes the visual because that is thought to be one way of attracting viewers. Television news is what it is for the same reasons that television itself in America is largely entertainment.

Walter Cronkite repeatedly has called network news a headline service. He is right, but with one qualification. The headlines are told as tales of conflict—stories that at their most adroit involve the viewer in drama. The news of the world and the nation is not announced, but recounted as synopses suitable for fiction, with a precipitating event, forces arrayed in opposition, and at the end tentative resolution. Whether it is man against nature, God, or other men, television news gives structure to events.

Many years ago, two sociologists in Chicago documented television's tendency to impose its own order on events. The occasion was "Mac-Arthur Day" when the general visited the city following his dismissal as commander of U.S. forces in the Korean war. Kurt and Gladys Lang stationed observers at the airport, along the parade route, and at Soldiers Field where MacArthur was to give an evening speech. To many, Mac-Arthur was an abused hero; to others, a military man who was ready to ignore civilian leadership in pursuit of victory. He was spoken of as a presidential candidate, and later would deliver an emotional address to a joint session of Congress. The observers found the crowds desultory and motivated by the possibility of a spectacle. Fascination with MacArthur as a figure of ideology was absent. Television conveyed a different picture— excited, seething crowds; adoration of the hero; attentiveness and awe. Television gave coherence where it was lacking and in accord with the expectations about the event that the mass media had created. Television created its own MacArthur Day in which the general was the center of partisan attention. Television journalists were proud of their dramatic coverage. In effect, the general received a hype—motivated not by ideology but by the demands of the medium.

Two political scientists more recently have recorded a departure by television from the reality experienced by participants. David Paletz and Martha Elson interviewed delegates to the 1972 Democratic Convention on the congruity between the impressions conveyed by coverage of earlier conventions and their own experience. The delegates recalled that television had emphasized demonstrations, hoopla, and the excitement of the convention floor; they found their role to be far more businesslike, with more time devoted to meetings and serious work than television had led them to expect. Serious work does not make an interesting picture.

Tom Patterson and Robert McClure, political scientists, similarly have raised questions about the dedication of television news to visual storytelling. They found that the viewing of national news during a presidential campaign made no contribution to voter knowledge of issues. Ironically, such knowledge did seem to be increased by exposure to partisan, paid-for telecasts and commercials. These researchers attribute the failure of network news to be informative to the emphasis on the visual and the dramatic within the very limited time alloted to the news. Paid-for telecasts sometimes increase knowledge precisely because they occasionally convey something new. What is diverting may well be redundant informationally.

It is hardly surprising, then, to find that newspapers appear to be more effective in formulating priorities among their readers than television is among its viewers. Most people pay some attention to each, and both often emphasize the same things. But when differences in attention and emphasis have been detectable, it is newspapers that seem to be more influential. This perspective singles out topic instead of partisan influence as an effect of the media—not what people think, but what they come to think about. Maxwell McCombs, a communications researcher, has labeled it the "agenda-setting function" of the press. Television may be comparatively weak in this respect not only because it fails to provide much that is new about issues, but also because its visuality, ever-present drama, and brevity may confuse viewers about the varying importance that has been assigned to stories. Conversely, newspapers undoubtedly owe some of their agenda-setting effectiveness to their greater popularity among the better-educated—who are better able to understand what is reported in depth and somewhat more likely to be attuned to the conventions of journalistic emphasis, such as story length, placement, and headline size.

Television news is also what it is because broadcasting has been regulated by the federal government. The Fairness Doctrine requires a "reasonable" amount of attention to public issues and a "reasonable" parity for opposing viewpoints. Over the years, the FCC has made it clear that news programs are the expected means of fulfillment and that national issues cannot be ignored. Thus, the public service obligation that broadcasters must meet to retain their licenses has come to include not only "news" but "national news." The result has been (1) to create a market among stations for news—in particular, national news; (2) to encourage a news style among the networks and other vendors in which stories are translated whenever possible into national news (the event in Oshkosh becomes a symptom of wider malignance); and (3) in behalf of balance, to make of many stories an account of two opposing parties.

The news market, of course, is no more demanding than dictated by FCC censure and profits. Thus, as the 1970s came to a close, we found network affiliates strongly resisting the expansion of time devoted to network news. The rationale: Revenue to the stations would be reduced by receiving a share allocated by a network instead of programming and selling the time themselves. The headline service remained no more than that. Complex issues and their interpretation received no relief from the conspiracy of the Fairness Doctrine, time, and television's urge for popularity. Television news often ignores the subtle diversities that mark public opinion because their recognition is unnecessary—two vivid viewpoints, whatever their merits or representativeness, will satisfy the reigning deities.

Certain tribulations of television news operation, in conjunction with the imprecation of economizing, similarly shape television news. Transmission lines are expensive; camera crews are more available in the cities where there are major television stations. Coverage is cut to fit this cloth. The ideal news day is well planned so that events, reporters, and cameras converge; events that can be scheduled in advance will be preferred—which means nonevents, such as interviews, announcements, and the bestowing of honors.

Alexander Cockburn, the caustic *Village Voice* columnist, some years ago noticed that American newspapers often give only an inch or two to the freak deaths of hundreds in Africa or Asia. He proposed a scale of equivalence for the value of human life based on the column inch. Americans would surely rank first, presumably followed by western Europeans. The values of television news operation can be similarly mocked. We may imagine the point at which deaths, catastrophe, or threatening events appear almost equal in news value to what has been conveniently scheduled. Only when they pass this threshold do they become news.

Journalists like to justify their decisions on the grounds of professional standards and the duty of the news to reflect events. They are right in recognizing that news reporting as an occupation carries with it a set of values by which events are judged, but they are wrong to apply to themselves the term professional. News values emphasize the unusual, the bizarre, the attraction of public attention equally with social and political significance, and beating the opposition equally with accuracy. Journalists, like any group of skilled practitioners, play to each other first, for naturally their peers are assumed to be the best judges of news. They cannot properly claim professionalism as a shield as can doctors and lawyers because job entry is not contingent on training and examinations. Journalists generally do value accuracy and fairness and, on the whole, they may serve society better when they have special privileges, such as the right not to disclose sources when called as a witness in court. They surely may display as much honor, bravery, cunning, and skill as might anyone else in behalf of their values. What the concept of news values does not do is seal the news from criticism. News values do not explain why the media are different in their treatment of the news, and they are not values to which it is necessary to subscribe for the sake of an informed public.

Journalists are not everything their rhetoric would claim, but neither are they the proper target of criticism. News *is* manufactured, and there are often good reasons to be dissatisfied with the product, but the blame usually does not lie with the newsgatherer. It is more frequently found in the institution of news itself and in the needs of the various media. *News from Nowhere* is the label applied by Edward Jay Epstein; it has struck many as perfect.

RISE OF A MEDIUM

One of the biggest stories of the past 30 years about the media has been the rise in public imagination of television as a news source. It has usurped and outdistanced every rival in every conceivable way in respect to public esteem, broadly conceived. Newspapers, magazines, and radio, once alone in competition, for awhile were variously judged as superior to television. No longer.

Whether we draw on those surveys of public opinion a decade apart by Steiner and by Bower or on a series of public opinion polls continuing up to the present by The Roper Organization, we are led to the same conclusion. Television upon first thought is the public's preeminent news medium. It is even accorded superiority at tasks at which it would seem certain to fall second.

When asked about news sources, a majority of the public today will name television as providing *most* of its news. In 1960, a majority would have named newspapers. Television is also the leader by a substantial margin in credibility when media accounts conflict; for being *quickest* with the *latest* news; and for being the *fairest* and *least biased* of the media. In 1960, newspapers would have led for credibility and lack of bias and radio would have been first for rapidity of dissemination. The competition is only close for completeness of coverage; nevertheless, here television today is rated first by more people than are newspapers.

In each of these cases, television's rise in public esteem has been accompanied by a comparable decline in the evaluation of the media providing the most direct competition—newspapers and radio, as sources of most news; newspapers, as most credible, complete, and unbiased; radio, as the most rapid disseminator. And it has occurred in part in contrast to the facts, for radio remains the most rapid disseminator, as exemplified in flood and hurricane announcements, and presidential assassinations and resignations, and newspapers in few cases could be said to be less complete in coverage than television.

The dominance of television news is both illusion and fact. There is no doubt that "television" is foremost when the public thinks about the "news." And this is where fact becomes appearance. Television has become synonymous with news because the term "news" connotes the national events in which the networks specialize. When asked about "the news," "television" precedes newspapers, radio, and magazines as a symbol. The fact is that television is undeniably first as a symbol, but far from clearly so in the facts of news delivery.

When the public is asked about specific news stories rather than "news," or directed away from national events toward regional, state, and local stories, the status accorded newspapers increases. Often in such circumstances newspapers receive the greatest public acclaim. The fact that local television news generally attracts an audience of about the same size as national news and treats its local events about as well and colorfully but fails to achieve comparable public approval, reinforces the belief that the standing of "television news" represents more what is in the mind than actually before the eye of the public.

Sociologist Mark Levy asked several hundred adults in Albany, New York, to name their sources of news. Television was far less often cited for local than for national and international news; newspapers were first for local news and close to television for national and international news. However, more than a fourth of the sample named both newspapers and television as equally important sources for both kinds of news. Again, a more subtle analysis than simply comparing first choices among the media reduces the significance of television.

We are still dealing with opinions. Behavior now confirms our suspicions. John Robinson, the public opinion analyst, examined the media-use diaries of several thousand Americans. These diaries, collected in advertising research, recorded two phenomena that are astounding in light of what the public says about television news. More than half of the adults did not watch a single national news program in a two-week period. On the average day, three times as many adults read some part of a newspaper than viewed some portion of the evening network news. In 1977, the average daily adult readership of newspapers was 104 million, the average weekly adult readership of *Time, Newsweek,* and *U.S. News and World Report* combined was 47 million, but the average nightly audience viewing network news was only 34 million. Thus, all data about media use support the view that television news is not as important as people say it is.

Yet the impression given by superficial measurement of public opinion is not entirely wrong. Television actually does appear to have greater credibility than newspapers or other media. As greater specificity and care are applied to assessing public behavior, the quantitative contribution of television in news delivery becomes less; not so for credibility. Television remains the most credible of the media no matter how public opinion is measured.

This credibility is distinctly of television's own making. The absence of the partisan allegiances historically so common to newspapers surely plays a part. The brevity of stories that is so typical precludes detail that might trespass on fact or interpretation that would strain confidence. And at its heart are two features embodied in television—the visual coverage of events and the display of news personnel. These two are the reasons most frequently advanced by those who rate television as first in credibility. Those who rate newspapers first cite different reasons, such as completeness of coverage. This discrepancy in rationales hints not at differences on a single standard but the application of two different sets of values. Before television, no one would have attached such notions to credibility. Experience with television may be slowly reshaping the public's concept of truthfulness in news.

A simple tale, often mistold. Television is not as dominant a news source as many have too hurriedly concluded. Television enjoys extraordinary preeminence as the symbol of news. It is the most credible of the media. It is far less important as a news source than the replies of the public, carelessly examined, would lead one to believe.

WHO WATCHES

Evening network news exemplifies the predominance of entertainment in American television. When the ratings for each type of evening network program are averaged, using the program categories employed by the A.C. Nielsen Company, the result is a measure of the popularity of the format. When these average ratings are broken down by age and sex for each category of program, the result is a demographic profile of the audience for the format. News, by such criteria, does not fare well.

News is less popular than any entertainment format broadcast in the evening. Drama, suspense and mystery, situation comedy, variety, and feature films on the average all attract larger audiences than does the average national news program. More children under the age of 12 are watching throughout Saturday and Sunday mornings than there are adult households paying attention each evening to the national news.

The impression of a delimited audience becomes stronger when the profile for each format is examined. News, of course, is less popular among children and teenagers than any of the entertainment formats. It would be plausible to guess that the greater popularity of entertainment formats among all households is actually attributable, not to adults, but to these younger viewers. Not so. The entertainment formats are more popular among adults 18-49 years of age than is evening network news. Not one of these entertainment formats attracts, on the average, fewer of these adult viewers than the evening news. In some cases, they are half again or even twice as popular among such viewers. The news audience is also disproportionately older. In some cases, it is about as popular, and in others more popular, than the entertainment formats among viewers 50 years of age and older. This is why the commercials accompanying the news so often are in behalf of the more funereal of drug store and supermarket products—dental adhesives, pain relievers, stomach remedies, and various counteractants to the wear and tear of aging.

It is sometimes argued that the staggering of network news throughout the evening would better serve the public by making news more accessible.

The apparently limited appeal of news casts this enlightened-sounding proposal into darkness. Inevitably, some who do not now see the news would do so. Equally certainly, some who now view the news because there is nothing more bearable on television at that hour would neglect it entirely. The proportion of viewers led across the evening hours by the trail of entertainment very likely would exceed those for whom the news was newly accessible, and probably would be those least likely to use other news sources. Greater access in the television schedule would not necessarily mean greater attention across the country.

BIAS AND BALANCE

A sizable proportion of the public believes that network television news is biased. The precise proportion depends on the wording, and possibly the timing, of the query. Generally, about a fourth to a third of the public will agree that network news favors conservatives or liberals or is somehow distorted. These critics, however, are unable as a group to give any hint of the direction of the bias, and as individuals they apparently are able to some degree to find compatible newscasters.

The poll sponsored a few years ago by *TV Guide* is typical. James Hickey found that about a third of the national sample of 2,000 adults endorsed the view that television news was "more biased than ... objective." Yet, focusing on the direction of bias, he discovered no majority opinion. About a fourth perceived some bias in favor of the governing Nixon Administration, and about a fourth perceived bias against it. About 12 percent each perceived the Democrats and the Republicans as receiving more favorable treatment. Sixteen percent perceived bias favoring liberals; 14 percent perceived bias favoring conservatives. More perfect balance would be hard to achieve.

Bower, in his 1970 national survey, found that slightly more than a fourth of the public endorsed the view that as a group television reporters "color the news." About 10 percent agreed that some do, some don't. Slightly more than half thought television reporters "give it straight." Bias was about equally perceived by people describing themselves as conservative, middle-of-the-road, or liberal. Of the total sample, only six percent thought their preferred reporter distorted the news. Even among those attributing bias to television reporters in general, more than half believed their preferred reporter did *not* "color the news."

The consequence of all this—the lack of concensus about the direction of bias and the large proportion of those critics who can find at least one television reporter who does not distort—is that there is no substantial dissatisfaction with the fairness of television news. The faultfinder who can command the public ear because of his prominence can find plenty of people who will agree with him temporarily, but, as with commercials and with effects on children, there are too many crosscurrents in public opinion for it to be effectively marshaled against television.

Over the years there have been many objective, empirical analyses of network news content. These examinations differ from the critical assessments of individuals, no matter how well documented or how specific, by their care in sampling newscasts so as to ensure representativeness, and their use of procedures that minimize the role of subjective factors. Some have recorded coverage as it was broadcast, but most have used videotapes, and such scrutiny of the news has been immensely aided by the news archives at Vanderbilt University and George Washington University where videotapes of all network coverage are available for review.

Such investigations are invaluable for fairly assessing the performance of television news because they are the sole sources of information that go beyond impressions and partisanship. Nevertheless, they do not translate readily into conclusions about bias. Human judgment must first be applied to the objective record.

The difficulty—and it is one that must be understood if foolish conclusions are not to be drawn—lies in the nature of news itself and the expectations we have of it in our society. Bias presumes the distortion of events. News itself as the product of the application of news values to events cannot help but be selective and interpretive; it is never simply a mirror of reality. News coverage can only infrequently be compared against the events themselves. More commonly, the only standard for assessing the performance of a journalist or a news medium is coverage by another source. There is not often a good reason for assuming that one source is superior to another. News sources can be compared, but the identification of one or another as more truthful, except in simple matters of fact, is always problematical.

Balance is another matter. It is fairly easy to determine whether accounts are balanced with respect to issues, political parties, personages, and groups in conflict. Balance can be examined in terms of time devoted to one or another viewpoint or person, or the proportion of statements that may be said to be favorable, unfavorable, or neutral in describing them. It can be applied to questions of camera treatment. The weight or importance accorded different components of public life, such as international news, domestic crime, health care, defense, and energy, can similarly be evaluated. Bias, however, cannot readily be inferred from imbalance. News is supposed to emphasize the significant. Disproportionate emphasis does not necessarily mean bias; it may only reflect astute judgment in reportage.

For example, in the 1972 presidential campaign the incumbent, Richard Nixon, adopted the strategy of presenting himself as president. Network attention to the Democratic and Republican nominees *as candidates* was greater for George McGovern. He made more partisan appearances than Nixon, while the Republican campaign employed surrogates in behalf of the President. In addition, the Democratic senator undeniably made news with his tribulations over discarding his vice-presidential choice for Sargent Shriver, former head of the Peace Corps, when it was revealed that Thomas Eagleton had a history of shock treatment for mental illness. Total network attention, however, was somewhat greater for Nixon because he received considerable coverage in fulfilling the duties of President.

Similar ambiguity in regard to bias is exemplified by the network coverage of the U.S. invasion of Laos early in 1971 during the Vietnam war. Several senators attacked the networks for portraying the United States unfavorably, much as Spiro T. Agnew a year before had attacked them for emphasizing news unfavorable to the Nixon Administration. Richard Pride and Gary Wamsley, two political scientists, analyzed the coverage by ABC and CBS over three months. They classified statements about the United States, South Vietnam, and North Vietnam as favorable or unfavorable in regard to two topics, military strength and morality. The two networks were similar in coverage except that CBS was somewhat more negative than ABC about U.S. strength. Both were much more positive than negative about the military strength of North Vietnam. Neither had much to say about the morality of North or South Vietnam, and were roughly balanced in the positive and negative portrayal of U.S. morality.

In both instances, there is imbalance. Yet the nature of the Nixon-McGovern campaign, and the lack of success for the U.S. invasion of Laos, do not encourage the label of bias. Events in these instances seem to be consistent with coverage. The lack of an objective standard of truth, and the expectation that news should vary with significance, makes the imputing of bias a task for subtlety and care.

Every story, of course, presents new opportunities for journalistic distortion. Empirical analyses pertain only to the past and to the particular coverage analyzed. The empirical record, however, provides no solace to those who would claim that network news has embodied strong liberal or conservative partisanship.

Polemicist and former *TV Guide* writer Edith Efron challenged the integrity of television news by purportedly documenting extensive bias favoring liberal positions and the Democratic candidate, Hubert Humphrey, in the 1968 presidential campaign. She called her book *The News Twisters*. She quickly became the focus of discord that embraced not only the quality of television news but the partisan forces upon which the news reflected. If the news were unfavorable to conservatives, liberals could hardly tolerate the label of bias any more than conservatives would accede to its inappropriateness. No one could doubt that by her arithmetic there was extreme imbalance. Robert Stevenson, a journalism professor, led a reanalysis of the videotapes for one network, CBS. Efron had ignored neutral content and had relied on the plausibility of her definitions of bias to justify their application. Stevenson, who asserted he was "Untwisting *The News Twisters,*" was more thorough. He included neutral content, and he made sure that people could agree on the application of his definitions. He found that Humphrey and Nixon each received more favorable than unfavorable treatment and in almost equal proportion. More importantly, he recorded about two-thirds of the news coverage as neutral.

There is an important lesson here. Neutral content cannot be ignored in evaluating news performance, for a ratio of favorability toward one or another side depends for its importance on the context in which it appears. Two statements for, one statement against, and 997 neutral tell a different story than 667 statements for, 333 against, and none neutral. Senator Robert Dole similarly had erred in attacking the Laos coverage for the small proportion favorable to the United States and South Vietnam. More than half the coverage was neutral; in this context, the senator's complaint, even if literally true, shrivels in significance.

So far the many studies of presidential campaign coverage portray television as even-handed ideologically. Perfect balance would never be expected. Emphases and attention inevitably will shift in response to the campaign; efforts at balance will be compromised by other news values. The best we can hope for is coverage that does not seem uniformly one-sided or thoroughly inconsistent with the way a campaign has unfolded.

Richard Frank, a political analyst, pursued the subtleties and shifts in coverage as a campaign unfolds about as sensitively as empiricism permits. He subjected seven weeks of nightly newscasts selected to represent the beginning, middle, and end of the 1972 campaign to the scrutiny of a team of four coders. These four classified each political story on 29 different dimensions, including duration of air time, issue or topic, hard versus soft news, and camera treatment. The coders attempted to encompass such niceties as the portrayed friendliness of the crowds Nixon and McGovern faced.

What emerges is a picture of coverage varying from network to network presumably as the consequence of different news policies. The campaign would have evolved differently for a patron of one or another of the networks; again, the fact that news invariably creates a second reality rather than merely conveying what took place is inescapable. NBC gave more attention to the Vietnam war. ABC and NBC were more favorable to Nixon than to McGovern; CBS was more favorable to McGovern than to

Nixon. ABC and NBC reported equal numbers of embarrassing stories for both parties; CBS reported two stories embarrassing to the Republicans for every one embarrassing to the Democrats. About 80 percent of all stories were reports of events (hard news), but the emphasis on background and the analysis of trends (soft news) varied as the campaign progressed. ABC and NBC decreased soft news as the campaign progressed; CBS emphasized soft news more, and increased it during the campaign.

Television news portrayed a government of one dominant branch and two indolent ones. There were over 300 stories where action was attributed to a branch of government. In 56 percent, it was the executive branch. The legislative branch was depicted as taking some action in only 25 percent, and the judicial branch in 18 percent. The unstated story apparently was that U.S. government is the president.

Nixon and McGovern proved to be different subjects for the medium. McGovern more often was held in close-up. He was portrayed more frequently before an audience. He more often declared his political convictions. He received far more minutes on camera. The Nixon strategy of presenting himself as the nation's dignified leader kept him from the rostrum and the sharp statement. One is left wondering about the appeal of McGovern's face. One cannot help but be impressed with the many ways that television can doctor its second reality—so many more than a newspaper with nothing other than words, type, and photographs.

Frank reached two conclusions. There had been "wide news reporting diversity, both among and within networks over different message dimensions and news topics." Despite this diversity, there had been no pronounced bias.

Complexity was at the heart of Frank's analysis. He translated into empirical terms the obvious fact that television coverage may vary in many ways, and in finding little consistency in favorability toward either of the candidates across his many message dimensions concluded that bias was not a just label.

C. Richard Hofstetter, a political scientist, construed the same 1972 election in very different terms. He used diversity itself as a measure of partisan bias. Hofstetter analyzed the nightly stories and minutes of political coverage by the three networks for 17 weeks prior to the election. Frank's solution to the absence of a standard against which the coverage of events could be measured for fairness was the sheer quantity of his news dimensions—29. He reasoned that favorability should be consistent across most before bias could be inferred. Hofstetter took a different stance: He reasoned that because news is a reconstruction of a reality that almost always will be beyond the experience of viewers or readers, and generally beyond that of any one or few reporters, news must become its own criterion. He proposed that political bias could be thought of as occurring when there was a noteworthy deviation among the networks in favorability toward a party or candidate. He then argued that bias of a second sort is inevitable precisely because the media cannot merely transmit events. For this kind of distortion he proposed the term "structural bias" to represent the idea that it emanated from the character and operating circumstances of a medium. It would be detectable when television as a whole differed in its coverage from the thrust of newspapers or magazines. Political bias would be reflected in diversity across networks; structural bias in similarity diverging from the coverage typical of other media.

This ingenious scheme led Hofstetter to two conclusions. His analysis convinced him that there was observable structural bias in 1972 campaign coverage. Television told its own story. However, he found only modest differences among the networks in their favorability toward either of the parties or toward Nixon and McGovern. Political bias, he judged, was not present.

Diversity by itself is neither good nor bad. Diversity in favorability might betray bias; it could represent the fair-minded application of somewhat different news values. It becomes bias only when someone labels it so, and backs up the label with a cogent argument. Diversity in stories covered, emphases, and treatment will only reflect differing values. As something that might be sought for itself, diversity is ambiguous. The principle behind having more than one news source is not diversity, but the protection the possibility of diversity provides. Multiple sources decrease the likelihood that the media can be the instrument of propaganda, or that important news will escape attention. Competition is supposed to spur integrity, not necessarily differences.

Cynics often mock television for the sameness of the coverage by the three networks. Yet it would be profoundly disturbing to find them so different that the news seemed to represent three planets. Certainly the public does not entirely agree that coverage is identical, or those perceiving bias in much of television reportage would not find it absent in their preferred reporter. The facts of the matter are that the networks converge to a substantial degree, yet also differ enough so that it is fair to say that they constitute three distinct voices.

James Lemert, a communications researcher, several years ago analyzed the degree of overlap among the networks over a two-month period. He found that about six out of 10 stories were carried by all three networks. Seventy percent were carried by at least two. Most of the overlap occurred for hard news; diversity occurred for background, interpretation, and features. These figures probably fairly represent the commonality of coverage in any year at any time, except when events of overriding importance would increase convergence. What they tell us is that the standards of journalism are authoritative, but not dictatorial; a goodly proportion of news lies with the beholder.

There is no doubt that there are many measurable differences among the network newscasts. Lemert found fewer stories on ABC (17 per broadcast), most on NBC (21), with CBS (19) falling in between. Frank, of course, found considerable diversity; the more dimensions that are measured, the more likely it is that differences will appear. Hofstetter found little diversity, but he focused on distinct political favorability interpretable as bias, a tendency news personnel would try to avoid. Apparently, they were successful. Other analysts have uncovered diversity of various kinds. The networks have been found to be dissimilar in their attention to race relations and the student protest movement in the early 1970s. The degree of interpretation by anchor persons has been found to vary. Cataclysm, threat, suffering, and violence have not always been similarly emphasized.

Such variation justifies the continual soul-searching that is presumably part of news reporting. Variation is the product of decisions, some representing definite policies and others occurring happenstance. When the networks concur, there is security of numbers; judgments appear at least to represent the norm for the circumstance. There is the question of whether the norm is valid, but empirically it is fact. The reporter is right to think that he has done no more than any competent person in his place would do. When there is diversity, norms either are ambiguous or being violated. In such cases, standards cannot so easily be invoked as the source of behavior. At the very least, there has been an intervening step in their interpretation that has led to very different outcomes. There may be very many points from day to day when individuals will vary in the decisions they reach. If these decisions noticeably diverge over time, the news that flows to the public may require intensive scrutiny. They do not, by the fact of being dissimilar, become unjustified. What would be unjustified is that they should occur thoughtlessly, by accident, without acknowledgment, or in indifference to the lack of unanimity about the nature of news. Empirical analyses of news, then, serve two purposes beyond providing the factual basis for judgments of bias: They record the accepted norms of reportage, opening those norms to question, and they document the places where norms have been inadequate or, by accident or design, disregarded—thereby holding up these deviations for inspection.

POLITICAL INFLUENCE

Television has undeniably transformed American politics. It has altered the nominating conventions, changed the organization and style of presidential campaigns, and created a political environment distinct from the days when the major contenders would personally attempt to cross every state by train or plane. Television has helped weaken the influence of party leaders and party mechanisms at every level. It has increased enormously the vicarious participation of the public in politics, yet it has not changed that dictum of many years' standing that the mass media reinforce and crystallize opinion more often than they appear to change votes from one party to another.

Harold Mendelsohn and Irving Crespi, astute students of public opinion, have characterized the "new politics" as the conjunction of polls, computers, and television. Politicians now design their campaigns with detailed information on what the public thinks, carefully staking out positions that either take advantage of support or evade disfavor. It is a sorry candidate for the House, Senate, or presidency who does not quantitatively assess public sentiment. These private endeavors take place in a context in which the public polls, often financed by newspapers or by television, inform the world at any given moment of his likely success.

At the same time, television has become the principal means of appealing to the public. Television commercials carry to the voter the image thought to be most acceptable; scholarly, authoritarian, humane, democratic, vital, relaxed, youthful, mature, Polonius at speed. Television coverage is a principal determinant of campaign planning, with announcements, speeches, and activities designed to coincide with the schedule and needs of the medium. Television speeches, debates, and talkathons are the new centerpieces. Political success has come to depend on skill at manipulating information and on adroitness before the camera—two circumstances served best by money enough to buy the expertise that can bring them about.

The 1960 campaign initiated the television era in presidential politics. Richard Nixon adhered to the whistle-stop strategy—every state, 188 cities, 150 major speeches, 65,500 miles. About 10 million saw him. He used television for direct appeals only in the final days. John F. Kennedy focused on the major states thought to be undecided. He turned to television to confront the issue of Catholicism, using in 10 key states a 30-minute videotape of a question-and-answer session before Protestant ministers in Texas.

Then there were the four televised debates. Nixon, recovering from illness, prepared for them as if they would be won by the kind of arguments that had served him at Whittier College. Kennedy saw them as the chance to make not only his views but his vitality and magnetism known to the public. About 75 million, the largest television audience up to that time, saw the first debate.

Sociologists Elihu Katz and Jacob Feldman pieced together the impact of these encounters from 31 independent and different studies of viewer reactions. Only the first debate had a significant impact. The haggard Nixon was widely perceived as "losing." Kennedy became more favored by his supporters, less disliked by those favoring Nixon. Nixon lost comparably in public esteem. National polls suggest there may have been a trend toward Kennedy before the first debate, and the claim by journalists that the first debate won the election for him is presumptuous—but there is no doubt it helped, and in precisely the way Kennedy needed. Nixon as Vice President was well-known nationally, both within his party and by the general public. Kennedy was a relatively new face, an Easterner, a Catholic, for whom the arousing of support among Democrats nationwide, the majority in voter registration, was crucial. The first debate helped him achieve that. The studies also confirmed that Kennedy had perceived the debates correctly. Voters appeared to absorb more about the style of the men than about the issues. Kennedy used television artfully and as a component of a geographically focused campaign; Nixon appended it clumsily to traditional strategy. Practice follows victory in politics, and presidential campaigns would never again be the same.

Nixon in 1968 behaved differently. He was televised throughout the campaign before selected, friendly audiences. Hubert Humphrey, already placed at a disadvantage by the coverage of the rioting and discord at the Chicago convention, found his coverage filled with strident anti-Vietnam-war hecklers. It is ironic that Nixon learned so slowly, since he had used television masterfully in 1952 with his "Checkers" speech in which his dog, Pat's cloth coat, and his mortgage were invoked before 25 million viewers to dispel public suspicions over an $18,235 expense fund privately provided him by a small group of Californians. After Nixon's closing appeal for support brought thousands of letters, wires, and calls to the Republican National Committee, Dwight D. Eisenhower embraced him with the words, "You're my boy!" Eisenhower had weighed dropping him as a running mate; Nixon's performance, by making the effect of rejection on Republican success ambiguous, apparently left the General, always eager to appear conscionable, unable to distinguish among right, wrong, and the demands of his new mission. Nixon should have realized then that television's strength is its ability to suggest trait, manner, and personality, for the success of this program, prepared by an advertising agency, rested on its portrayal of a man of ordinary honesty unfairly rebuked in his pursuit of the American dream—a theme left not to words but to his desertion in mid-speech of the protection of his desk and Pat's devoted expression.

By the late 1960s, the pattern of the television era had become established. The conventions were covered as news and entertainment. Spots and short programs became more prominent, lengthy speeches less so, among paid-for broadcasts—for the longer the political broadcast the greater the drop in audience from what would have been expected for entertainment. Spots showed no more deficit than commercials of any type. Furthermore, as studies were still demonstrating in the 1970s, they overcome the selective exposure by which persons disinterested in politics or unfavorable to a candidate will avoid a scheduled appeal. In 1956, 85 percent of presidential campaign television expenditures had gone for speeches; three elections later, with total expenditures four times greater, such major presentations occupied only half the budgets. Nevertheless, the speech and other long programs remained important as symbol and as punctuation mark for the campaign. They merely became recognized as having the more limited purpose of assembling the interested and the loyal, thereby increasing the likelihood that they would remain that way.

Television has changed the nominating conventions from deliberative, if volatile, bodies to orchestrated showcases. This has come about in several ways. By opening the conventions to the television viewer, politicians have become fearful of offending anyone by what transpires. The function of television as entertainment cannot be ignored, as the parties wish to hold as many viewers as possible for the display of the nominee and his running mate. Inoffensive, contrived excitement is packaged. When that is what the parties offer, television can only conspire in its transmission in as dramatic a manner as possible, for the medium shares a goal with the party—a large, attentive audience.

The transformation has been hastened by what television has done to the primaries and by the journalistic machinery assembled by television for convention coverage. By focusing attention on the primaries as if each were *High Noon* again and again, the role of negotiation among party leaders in selecting a candidate has been reduced. For delegates and leaders alike less remains to be decided or bargained for at the conventions. By the eve of the convention, the field is usually narrowed to two contenders, one of whom often is already acknowledged as the victor. Once the convention is under way, television covers it as no lone newspaperman in a trenchcoat ever could. The literally hundreds that are arrayed by each network are so thorough in collecting information that little occurs that does not fit television's own prognostications. The 1976 Republican convention exemplifies the conversion of drama to anticlimax. Gerald Ford and Ronald Reagan were each within a few votes of the nomination. It was one of the closest convention contests of the century. Yet no viewer could doubt that Ford would be the nominee because television long before the vote had tracked down and verified the choice of every delegate. As the vote approached, the very few delegates who remained undecided became temporary celebrities. Everyone's choice had become a public commitment; a change would require recanting. By the time of the uproarious and emotional Reagan demonstration, his supporters were losers in charade entertaining the viewers.

Neither convention dazzlement nor seduction by spot, of course, were the main goal. The first lost the disinterested and the opposed; the second, as a commercial, could not help but suffer in credibility. From the first primary to election day, what the presidential candidates wanted most was to be included in regular network news. Favorable or neutral news coverage promised the maximum benefits of media exposure.

Edwin Emery, a journalism professor, succinctly characterizes the trends that had emerged by the 1970s:

> It seemed clear that despite the heavy expenditures to buy time on television and radio, the really desired goal was to obtain exposure on news programs. And the ultimate goal for presidential candidates was to have two or three minutes' coverage on a network evening show anchored by a Walter Cronkite, John Chancellor, or Harry Reasoner. Here, with substantial audiences of mixed political preferences and characteristics, the personality and the message of the candidate might become noticed by people who had not been reached through print media, direct mail, or interpersonal communication. The novelty of the 1976 presidential primaries, financed in part by federal matching funds and flushing out a crowded Democratic party entry list, brought methodical media attention to the "weekly primary vote" not unlike the attention paid to the weekly golf tournament. Daily reports, smash play on election day, analysis the day after, and human interest stories all added up to extensive media exposure for the winners—and rapid elimination for the despairing losers [Emery, 1976: 93].

Emery also documents a phenomenon that could escape someone without a sense of history and irony. By 1976 the whistle-stop campaign had returned, but in a new guise—and it had been brought back by television. Emery records that in 1976 the primaries were almost uniformly won by the candidate who expended the most effort, time, and money. These were contentious primaries, the Democrats narrowing a large field to Jimmy Carter and the Republicans oscillating between Ford and Reagan. In almost every case the winner spent big, devoted a sizable portion of the budget to brief appeals on radio and television, and trekked from factory to community to news conference in a way that attracted continual television news coverage. By the prominence it had given the primaries, television had made the handshake and the personal chat again a part of national politics, but now these were associated with the elimination rather than the final contest.

Nevertheless, television during the primary and presidential campaigns seldom can be identified as *the* factor responsible for a voter's decision. There are very sound and understandable reasons for this. Television is only one source of information, and it must compete with information from friends and family and from other media. Voting itself is a behavior that often follows past practice—those who have voted in the past are far more likely to vote again, and any prior consistency in party loyalty is very likely to be repeated. The candidates in many cases will make equally adept use of television; news coverage gives roughly equal treatment at least to the major candidates and to the two major parties. The mass media in news, and television in both news and political commercials, undoubtedly overcome selective exposure—the inclination of persons to avoid communication antithetical to their partisanship—because so much simply cannot be avoided if one pays attention at all. Selective perception—the interpretation of what is experienced in accord with predispositions—nevertheless will often operate, and selectivity certainly will preclude immersion in anything extensive or substantial conveying an unwelcome or irrelevant perspective. *King,* the NBC homage to the black civil rights leader, belied its presence on a mass medium in 1978 by attracting less than 10 percent of white viewers, while two-thirds of black households watched. Television undoubtedly has a larger role as a factor in persuading voters during the primaries than in the presidential election itself, because loyalties among the contenders are generally less strong, if they are present at all.

During the presidential campaign television has an important role, but it cannot often be said to switch a voter permanently from one candidate to another. The televised coverage of the conventions, following that of the primaries, focuses the nation's attention on the electoral task. Television news coverage and political commercials during the campaign help to maintain voter interest and support. However, their opportunity to influence voter choice between the two major parties is limited by the fact that in the typical election about 80 percent of the voters will have made a choice by the end of the conventions, and at least a fifth of those undecided will return to whatever party they have tended to favor in the past. Thus, television's principal role, as it is for all media, is to facilitate and encourage—but not to remake—voter decisions.

 Television, newspapers, and other mass media probably have their major influence between campaigns by establishing the framework within which elections are contested. The shaping of political attitudes is cumulative and slow. Campaigns are excitement and drama, building on what has gone before. They are also periods of public discount and skepticism, and the slowing or cessation of governmental and congressional activity. Watergate became an issue after the election of 1972 with new revelations, but their occurrence depended on a Congress back at work and their public reception on the atmosphere of postelection credibility.

 Major events, of course, remain a means by which the media may have great impact, both during and between campaigns. The ordinary flow of news is the slow drip that over decades leaves an impression. Big news that everyone comes to talk about is sometimes another matter—a shift in the economy or in foreign relations that seems to justify controversial policies, a bold stroke such as Nixon's surprise 1971 visit to mainland China or Jimmy Carter's 1979 achievement of some degree of agreement in the Middle East. In such circumstances, where the making of news and the manipulation of the media for political advantage converge, an incumbent president, or whoever in a particular contest holds high office, has a decided advantage, for he possesses the power to act. An incumbent is also better placed to ride the prevailing winds. Carter in 1980 not only benefited as a candidate from the support he received as president in the Iranian hostage crisis, but he avoided campaigning during the crisis on the grounds that his presidential obligations took precedence. Nixon had employed a similar strategy of presenting himself as president first, candidate second, in his 1972 contest with George McGovern.

Big news during a campaign nevertheless will be limited in influence by the partisanship already aroused and the commitments toward which voters are settled or leaning. Not only Watergate, but the Thomas Eagleton affair and McGovern's major televised speech on Vietnam in 1972 appeared to have scant effect on voters. In fact, Harold Mendelsohn and Garrett O'Keefe, in an intensive analysis of a panel of voters in Summit County, Ohio, found that more Nixon than McGovern supporters watched the McGovern speech presumably to confirm their rejection of his policies. This is certainly "selective exposure," but counter to the conventional meaning of the term; it is definitely selective perception.

The facilitative function is probably particularly strong for television because it emphasizes the visual and dramatic so much and is so relatively inept at conveying information about issues. Newspapers, because they can cover any topic in greater depth, are generally greater factors in instructing the public about the issues themselves. Yet television often figures importantly in the process by which voters finally confirm their inclinations at the polls. Besides helping to maintain interest and loyalty, when circumstances are ambiguous, television, by its cinematic power to convey to the viewer the candidates as living men, may assist him in acknowledging his preference. This capability of television is illustrated by the several thousand Pennsylvania voters studied by William Lucas and William Adams, political scientists, during the Ford-Carter election in 1976. This was an election in which there was extraordinary voter uncertainty, with as much as half of the electorate unclear about its choice a few weeks before election day. Lucas and Adams found that early decision-making by voters was associated with watching network news and with interpersonal conversations about the two candidates. Both of these factors were independently related to the reaching of an early decision, and Lucas and Adams reason that each had the similar function of giving the voters confidence about the correctness of their predilections. The "information" supplied by television in this instance was image; the direction of choice, not analyzed by Lucas and Williams, may not have been different than would have been predicted on the basis of voter background and voting history. However, the fact of decision rested in part on television.

Television is consistently cited by voters as their major source of campaign information. The findings of Mendelsohn and O'Keefe in Summit County during the 1972 Nixon-McGovern contest are typical. Throughout the campaign, one-half or more of the sample cited television as their principal source of information, with about a third or fewer naming newspapers, and a minute five percent naming other persons. As would be expected from the well-known beliefs of the public about the media, significantly more judged television to be "fair" than judged newspapers to be so. What these data mean is not that television is the foundation for choosing among candidates, or that in truth it is a more significant or important source than other sources, but only that it is a popular means by which people tune in to the political process.

The data from a variety of surveys, however, do not justify the conclusion that television is the most common means of informing the public about political campaigns. Besides the smallness, compared with the average audience for primetime entertainment, of the audience for network news and the greater frequency with which persons are likely to read a newspaper than view a network newscast within any given period of time, television news appears to be embarrassingly ineffectual, given the very large sums expended on nightly production, in informing voters. Patterson and McClure, of course, found that frequency of viewing the national news was unrelated to knowledge about issues. Journalism professor Peter Clarke and his colleague Eric Fredin give added credibility to the view that television news is intellectually inert. They examined exposure to newspapers and television news and the rationality employed by almost 1,900 voters representing a cross-section of the American public in their choice of a Senate candidate in 1974. Rationality was measured by the ability of the voters to state reasons for liking or disliking the candidates. The viewing of television news was negatively related to such rational decision-making, while the reading of newspapers was positively related to such behavior. Because they recognized that a reason that would qualify as rational for one person might be classified as irrational for another, they also analyzed media exposure and simple knowledge of the names of the candidates. The viewing of television news was unrelated to such basic knowledge, while the reading of newspapers was positively related to the possession of this information. These results are particularly striking because they reflect the associations between media use and rationality and knowledge independent of exposure to the medium not under scrutiny and independent of education and interest in politics. They are therefore

quite convincing in their message that among paper tigers television news is
indeed flimsy.

Those who believe that any new information will upset an established
pattern should examine the experience with the presidential election-day
coverage reaching voters in the west. It was thought by many that these
reports of east coast voting, which included predictions of the national
outcome, would alter the behavior of western voters who had not yet gone
to the polls. Several studies in the 1960s disconfirmed these fears: Neither
turnout nor voter choice were affected. In both elections in which such
reporting was examined, however, the eastern results matched voter expectations. Lyndon Johnson in 1964 had been expected to defeat Barry
Goldwater easily; the vote for Nixon and Humphrey in 1968 had been
expected to be close. Voters would already have discounted the likely
trend in making their decisions about voting and whom they would vote
for. Election day reporting counter to expectations would have unknown
effects. The perceived underdog might benefit by the arousal of previously
discouraged supporters; the perceived winner might benefit by warning
complacent supporters that all was not won. Conceivably, turnout would
rise without altering the net balance, or one or another candidate might
benefit disproportionately. The principle applies to communication in
general and illustrates why much of television political coverage has no
influence: Redundancy is essentially conservative or null in effect.

Newspapers and newsmagazines are disproportionately favored and
used as sources of information by the better-educated, white-collar em-
ployees, managers, members of the professions, and by those more intensely interested in the campaign. Nevertheless, television reaches a huge
and diverse public, and no one permanently can escape it the way he can a
particular newspaper or magazine. Television is the people's medium and
the one particularly relied upon by those who, for reasons of education,
income, or culture, have limited access to or make little use of other
sources—the poor, blacks and other minorities, and the elderly. These
groups, voluntarily or involuntarily, are more dependent on television, and
a sizable proportion is totally and involuntarily so. However, because of its
very character as a means of communication that must entertain, it is
limited in what it can convey. Television news must divert, too; public
issues are not always amusing. Television is the medium that reaches the
masses, but in the process by which it does so it sacrifices some of the
benefits that such wide appeal implies.

Viewers undeniably respond to television news in a way that rewards it
for being entertaining. Sociologist Mark Levy found in questioning news
viewers that diversion (news is funny, different, satisfies curiosity) and
emotional involvement (news is exciting, relaxing) were two major motives
for watching. About half of his sample of Albany, New York, adults

admitted they identified so closely with the newscasters that they felt sorry for them when they made a mistake. Other major motives were comprehension of events, mixed with a desire for reassurance about the state of the world and some relief from personal problems, and an interest in intellectual enrichment. These four motives—diversion, emotional involvement, comprehension mixed with reassurance, and enrichment—seemed to describe separate portions of the audience. A fifth set of viewers emphasized things that they thought were wrong with television news (exaggerates, redundant, superficial): Apparently, they watch to criticize. Television is thus well-advised to try to be entertaining with the news, for this approach adds to the audience. Besides whatever value such pleasure has for viewers, making the news entertaining could be advanced as a public service by attracting those who otherwise might pay no attention—but the price is its trivialization.

The penchant of television for diversion has caused many to think of it as diversionary. The most famous formulation of this view is the "narcoticizing dysfunction" proposed many decades ago by Paul Lazarsfeld and Robert Merton as the possible outcome of public absorption in the mass media. They speculated that attention to mass media news and entertainment might substitute for thoughtful and constructive action. A similar view is held by those who blame television for the decline in voter turnout in presidential elections that has continued since 1960.

The fact is that attention to the mass media consistently has been related to involvement in, not withdrawal from, political participation. Yet this does not at all rule out the possibility that television, through its influence on the conduct of politics, has helped to reduce voting. These are paradoxical trends, but they should not be wished away because they are difficult to reconcile.

Reinforcement and crystallization—the cultivation of predispositions and sharpening and elaboration of opinions already held—became the conventional wisdom about the political effects of the mass media as the result of studies of voting following World War II. These studies found that exposure to the mass media, which then meant newspapers, radio, and magazines, seemed to make a difference in the eventual choice of only a very few voters. Choice was largely predictable from region, religion, race, socioeconomic status, and party allegiance. Decisions made early in the campaigns left little opportunity for mass media influence. Close elections, then as always, might turn on any one of a myriad of factors, but the media typically did not seem to have a substantial influence.

Television, first present as a source of convention and campaign coverage and a vehicle for partisan appeals in 1952 when about one out of three households had a set, did not appear to alter this pattern. Yet circumstances, some encouraged by television, have changed the political status of the media. They are assuming a larger role than seemed plausible two decades ago.

Party allegiance has declined over the years. Issues have become more prominent in voter decision-making. Ticket-splitting is becoming more common, and party loyalty no longer is as powerful a predictor of voter choice. Early decision-making may become less common and stable, as exemplified in the Ford-Carter election. Information about issues and about the candidates themselves is coming to play a more important role during the campaign.

Television has contributed to these trends by weakening the role of party leaders and the party mechanism. Its coverage of the primaries has helped to do so in the contest for the presidency. In races for the House and the Senate, television has helped to do so by making it possible for candidates to appeal with greater force directly to voters; thus, they are less reliant on the support of the party.

Members of the House and Senate today are freer to ignore party positions in their voting and their stands on issues for the same reason—their reelection is less dependent on party support and more dependent on what they can communicate to the electorate, because of the access to television that money and cleverness ensure.

Television also provides a commanding stage for media events. The debates between Nixon and Kennedy and between Ford and Carter overcame the normal barriers that many people erect against political communication. The measure of their notoriety is that they become the substance for extensive coverage by other media—a trick none of *them* have been able to pull on television. The huge audiences drawn by these enshrined spectaculars approximated in size, diversity, and political apathy those for the Super Bowl. Their prowess lies not only in the status they achieve by being extraordinary, but in the fact that by simultaneously preempting all three networks they leave the television audience with little else to watch. Such presentations can expose the public to information that in any other form would be avoided. Television is different not simply because it presents talking pictures, but because of the audience only it can assemble.

The subtle way in which such media events may serve voters is illustrated by the 200 Wisconsin voters studied in 1976 by Jack Dennis and Steven Chaffee. Persons who ignored the Ford-Carter debates gave preeminence to party in their choice and needed no further information. Persons who watched all four debates changed more in their leanings during the campaign than either those who ignored the debates or those who watched irregularly, and they gave greater weight to issues. About a third of the voters were such persistent followers of the debates; for them image, although not irrelevant, figured as somewhat less important than for other, less searchful citizens. Apparently, television in this instance provided assistance to uncertain voters in making a choice.

Again, as in 1960, the various studies of the Ford-Carter encounters do not verify a net benefit in the final vote for either candidate unambiguously attributable to the debates; but in 1976, as in 1960, a significant portion of the electorate appeared to rely to some degree on this media event in reaching a decision. As in 1960 for Kennedy, there was a trend in the polls prior to the first debate favorable to Ford. Most of the influence attributable to the debates was confined to the first debate, which Ford was perceived as winning and from which he achieved an enhanced image in regard to his personal capabilities. Yet it can be argued that the winner of this election, who, like the one in 1960, was very close, was the participant who benefited most. This paradox results from the electoral inclinations of the public: Although Ford was able during the campaign to recover from a large early deficit in the polls, there were more voters who professed Democratic than Republican loyalties and more persons were leaning toward Carter initially. Carter, by making a generally favorable impression and being perceived the winner of the second and third debates, was able to solidify and maintain his support among those predisposed toward him.

The studies of the 1976 debates also provide insight into the particular role served in the campaign by such confrontations. Sears and Chaffee, as did Katz and Feldman for the 1960 debates, have identified the pattern they reveal. As he did for the earlier debates, the political communications specialist Sidney Kraus has assembled a historical account and a compendium of the empirical evidence in *The Great Debates, Carter vs. Ford, 1976.* Irony is the term that most consistently fits the findings. About 90 percent of the voters said that learning about the issues was their principal reason for giving attention to the debates, although about three-fourths also said they were interested in evaluating the candidates as individuals. Although one might be skeptical of whether issues in fact figured as strongly in motives as voters said they did, the performance of the press in covering the debates was a sorry one from the perspective of democratic theory. Trivialization describes their treatment of these events. Newspaper and television coverage gave only minute attention to what was said; instead, they concentrated on identifying the "winner" and on the drama associated with the two men meeting on the same stage. The actual proportions perceiving one or another as the winner after a debate were actually quite close, but after a few days of journalistic coverage the public much more decidedly came to view the initial narrow "victor" as the winner. Newspapers and television, by ignoring the issues, remade the debates.

As in 1960, the audience for the debates was huge when superficially measured, for over 80 percent of the public viewed some portion of them. However, a close examination of the data suggests that the proportion that could be said actually to have followed them was much more modest. Some tuned in but intellectually soon tuned out; such a relapse from initial resolve would be encouraged by the public's pervasive orientation toward television as a medium of entertainment and episodic attention. Some undoubtedly paid the scantest attention because their motive was simply to have something flickering in the room. Audience size declined for the second and third debates from the almost 75 percent that viewed at least some of the first encounter. Probably no more than about a quarter of the public followed any one debate closely, and probably about a quarter followed the entire series with a fair degree of consistent attention. Although the debates certainly reached many who ordinarily ignore political communication, attention to them was greatest among those who were best informed and least in need of additional information—those with a greater degree of education, greater interest in politics, and a greater level of participation in politically related activities. The status of television as the medium of national diversion was underscored by a *negative* relationship between average viewing of television and viewing of the debates, while reading of newspapers was positively related to viewing of the debates.

As in 1960, partisan affiliation was strongly related to perceiving which man emerged the winner. About two-thirds of those leaning toward a candidate at the time of each debate perceived him to be the winner. However, slight shifts upward and downward in this partisan unanimity, and the shifting judgments of those uncommitted, were sufficient to clearly establish a margin each time for one or the other of the candidates. Although the debates thus widely reinforced partisanship and this benefited Carter because of his initial advantage in support, there was some change possibly attributable to the debates in voter support, with about 13 percent of the electorate shifting in one poll between before and after the first debate; Ford in particular gained in areas with a high proportion of traditionally Republican voters. However, by election time voters seemed to remember very little of the debates, and the majority voted in accord with their predebate selections, although for a small minority the experience of the debates appeared to have affected their eventual choice.

The voters as a whole judged the debates to be worthwhile, but they also expressed disappointment in them. Ironically, those whose motive to view was to follow the excitement of the campaign, and not obtain information, were most satisfied. The implication is that the remaking of the debates in subsequent journalistic coverage deprived them of much of the value they might have had to the voters. Nevertheless, although in some samples voters tended to perceive the candidates as more alike after the debates, on the whole the evidence indicates that the debates, particularly the first one, sharpened the understanding of differences on issues between the candidates—an outcome which, given the emphases of subsequent journalism, must be attributed to the debates themselves.

The debates in 1960 and 1976 thus played a critical role in these elections. Although largely reinforcing predispositions and crystallizing opinion, they also offered to a few information necessary to reach a choice. In 1960, image seemed to be more affected than knowledge about issues; in 1976, with an electorate increasingly making issues the basis of its political choice, beliefs about the stands of the candidates on issues were as much or more affected. In 1976, both men were not well known by the public, neither possessed the dynamism of Jack Kennedy, and neither perpetrated the forensic blunders of Richard Nixon, and both Ford and Carter enhanced their personal images among the public.

The incentive for a debate is greatest for the candidate who is least known, has not established an image, or has not fully gained the commitment of those likely to support him. In 1960, Nixon was foolish to become involved in a debate. In 1976, Ford was the underdog, and Carter felt it necessary to prove his mettle. Before this second debate, a candidate could easily avoid entrapment in such an encounter without risking public disdain. One more debate and they will approach an institution—and one that candidates will reject at their peril. Television will have claimed another base for influence.

Close elections take on a somewhat different meaning when the electorate is unstable in its preferences. Ordinarily, the struggle is for the few who are uncommitted or uncertain. As party loyalties decline, more people become susceptible to persuasion at any given point in the campaign. As issues become more important, voters turn more to knowledge about the stands of candidates than to their party labels. In such circumstances, large numbers of voters in a close election may be susceptible to influence.

The implication of these varied changes in the political environment is that the influence of the mass media is increasing, for the foundation on which reinforcement must rest—loyalty—is not so clearly present. Even the basis for crystallization—opinion—may not be so often present because it no longer derives so directly from the position taken by a party. The position of television in this picture is problematical. Television news is not good at covering the issues: a headline service, actually entertainment, too visual, dramatic but not informative—whatever the precise phrase, the message is the same. It presents picturebook history. It does reach people who may disdain newspapers, even though newspapers on the whole may reach more people in the average day. Television has the best chance of reaching those who ignore politics; but such persons, low in interest, untouched by events, and generally indifferent to the news in any form, are the least likely to vote.

Why, then, is everyone so willing to acknowledge television as a powerful political medium? Perhaps this is due to its having engaged so visibly and in such a theatrical manner in the function that mass media have always served—the monitoring of politics. Perhaps it is because it *has* so changed the conduct of politics. Perhaps its status in public opinion as the preeminent news medium bestows a status on coverage that holds regardless of actual audience size. Politicians are well advised to seek television coverage, partly because, nationally, it is a medium with three voices at best (compared with the many more that make up newspapering), so that the audience assembled for a single message is beyond the capability of other media. For example, Chaim Eyal, a communications researcher, examined the emphasis given to various topics by the three networks and by newspapers in New Hampshire, Chicago, and Indianapolis, and found that the networks were almost identical but that the newspapers differed so much that one could not fairly speak of a newspaper portrayal of the world but only of the portrayal presented by a newspaper. Media events such as presidential debates dramatize this prowess, but it is continually at work. There is also something more: Television is not simply quantitatively important, but qualitatively different. The Checkers speech, the first Nixon-Kennedy debate, the readiness of those Pennsylvania news viewers to decide between Ford and Carter—these exemplify that capability of television to convey something about people beyond what they say or the acts which can be attributed to them. Yet television's pronounced devotion to entertainment, which enhances rather than conflicts with this contribution to image, also precludes the medium's domination of politics, for the trends have included a shift toward rationalism. For, contrary and paradoxical though it might seem, the weakening of party ties has been accompanied by the rise in importance of issues—the very matter that most eludes television.

4

ENTERTAINMENT AS INFORMATION

The imperfections of television as a news source do not exempt it from being a medium of information. Television is predominantly entertainment, and the means by which it diverts its audience inevitably also informs them. The tales of urban dishonesty, police procedure, and antic confrontation with the vicissitudes of job and sex in primetime vividly illustrate for their viewers experiences often unfamiliar and sometimes all too familiar, thereby bringing them news about the unknown and confirmation of the known. The noisy game shows and sagas of marital discord, moral lapse, and everyday evil that populate daytime television similarly function as pages from the book of life.

TALES OF TWO CITIES

Television has two capitals in America, New York and Los Angeles. Burbank, one of the seemingly endless municipalities that make up the balkan state of L.A., is as crowded with production companies and studios as the surrounding hillsides are dotted with houses of optimistic hues anomalously set among brave evergreens and palms. Deals big and small are closed in the coffee shop of the Sheraton-Universal in next-door Studio City while children wait impatiently for their parents to escort them to the repetitive mock disasters of derailing trains and snapping sharks just over the hill. Los Angeles is the factory of vicarious experience in the United States, a specialization in manufacture that began decades ago with silent movies and the Jewish merchants who found their star in the assembly of ideas and capital in pursuit of public adoration. They applied the principles of the dress business to entertainment, and found the fit good. New York, the second city by far in television and film production, is the business office and news headquarters of the medium. Within a few square blocks there are, at 54th Street and the Avenue of the Americas, that symbol of hemispheric congeniality referred to by taxi drivers as Sixth Avenue, the American Broadcasting Company in a bronze-sheathed tower across from the New York Hilton; a block away, at Fifty-Third Street, the Columbia Broadcasting System in a black granite-encased tour de force designed by Eero Saarinen for William S. Paley, where corporate autocracy is manifested in the barring of paintings, prints, and office decor unless they have official sanction; and, down the street and around the corner across from the skating rink, the National Broadcasting Company in Art Deco Rockefeller Center beneath the Rainbow Room. Here are the three networks, their presidents, their multitudinous staffs, and the endless luncheons, drinks, scheming, and planning that dictate the listings in *TV Guide*. What is thought in New York is what happens on the west coast, and eventually on the television screens across America.

These are our two greatest cities, rivaled only weakly by Chicago as a center of commerce and Washington as a center of government. Television, like our great newspapers and national magazines, is the work of urban men and women. They are people like many of us in many ways, yet they are different from most of those in the huge audiences whose attention they govern by their work. The mass media by their nature require people enarmored of the powers of the word, the image, and the idea as a commanding presence. Generalization, of course, is clumsy and likely to fit no one perfectly. The people who work in television certainly are diverse as a group, and they are so inevitably, for like those who function within any of our major institutions, they reflect to some degree the diversity that marks the rest of society. Yet they also share much that sets them apart: They are almost invariably highly competitive, bright, and clever; they are experts at using sentences and paragraphs as weapons to get their way; like the actors and personalities that appear on the screen, for whom "my face for the world to see" is an abiding motive, they often are driven toward the justification of their beings by the public acceptance of their ideas. Like horse-players, they live and die by the adequacy of their prognostications. They abide in a world where talent is a commodity whose value depends only in small part on brilliant expression and in large part on the revenues associated with popularity. They are likely to have a taste for shock, flamboyance, and the rupturing of complaisance, because audience attention and titillated dismay are the ventricles of show business, and for manipulation, which is equally at its heart. They frequently harbor the values of literature, which cares absolutely for expression and purpose and not at all for popularity, and of public service, which holds up goals of social justice and edification. As a consequence, they are also likely to find themselves often severely conflicted. For such ambitions, like those for the realization of their personal vision and the capturing of public fancy by outrage, cannot generally be achieved in a mass medium operated principally as a vehicle for advertising.

The powerful role of the values of show business is illustrated in the interviews conducted with members of the Hollywood television community by sociologist Muriel Cantor and by two journalism professors, Thomas Baldwin and Colby Lewis. Cantor interviewed about 60 producers of primetime television and 24 producers of children's television, focusing on their beliefs about their craft. Baldwin and Lewis interviewed about 40 producers, directors, and writers of primetime action series about the use of violence in television drama. What these people had to say about drama and cartoons is strikingly similar to what news personnel, in television and elsewhere, generally have to say about the news—the principal sources for their decisions are the conventions of the genre in which they work, the expectations of colleagues as to what will succeed and what is worthy, and the demands of the organizations (in this case, the networks) which are their clients. As news personnel prefer to think of themselves as servants to the rules set by the deity news, the Hollywood people see themselves as servants to the god entertainment. The children's producers applied simple principles of distraction and fast action acquired from their experiences in theater cartooning; what was acceptable was whatever would hold a child's transient attention. The younger producers, who had had little or no experience with other media, saw their audience as unsophisticated and, by comparison to themselves, rural; they had few compunctions about conforming to creative limitations imposed by the networks. They did not see themselves as conveyers of ideas, but as assemblers of skills and talents. Many of the older producers, who had had more varied media experience, saw themselves as creators of entertainment and chafed at restrictions that affected stories and casting because they believed such interference hampered their pursuit of popularity. What differentiated these two groups was not adherence to show business, but the acceptance by one and the rejection by the other of the conditions of its manufacture. A third group of older producers, many of whom also did considerable writing, opposed interference not because of its effects on popularity but because of its assumed threat to their ability to treat social and political issues. When the question was the use of violence, the Hollywood people explained that man against man is the most convenient conflict for resolution within the television format. Show business here requires a fast-moving story that peaks and recedes among the commercials before achieving a crescendo; physical combat, threat, weaponry fit. Television, whether it is Saturday morning or after school, primetime or daytime, comedy or action, game show or soap opera, is dedicated to the principle that gaining attention by whatever means is good. Social and political motives may create conflicts, and important ones, but they are minor as factors affecting the everyday business of making television.

The business offices and the production factories, centered 3,000 miles apart, both give their allegiance to popularity, but to a degree and in a manner sufficiently different that often they are pitted against each other. At root, it is the inevitable fray between the distributor and the craftsman. In careers in the mass media, there are forks at which one must choose between managing and making, judging and shaping. Those who choose the former route cannot help but sacrifice their creative urges to business judgments. What others create become in their hands products to be priced and peddled. Those who choose the second route cannot help but acknowledge, and in many cases become canny practitioners of, the business side of their business; yet business for them is constrained by, not always at peace with, and sometimes subservient to art and craft. Thus, newspaper and magazine publishers and advertising departments have separate interests from editors and writers, as to a lesser degree do the editors from the writers. In television, as in other media, these different interests are a matter of survival. The network president, the programming chief, the analysts of audience fealty and fickleness, seek to fill a schedule whose popularity will justify peak advertising rates. The producer, the director, and the writer are in accord that popularity is not irrelevant, but they often differ on its substance and the means of its achievement. The motives that directed them into the making of television levy a concern for the quality as well as the quantity of audience response. They see their work cheapened when it cannot emerge as they believe the principles of storytelling demand. They are often ready to settle for a smaller audience of many rather than maximum millions in behalf of the integrity of their work. In other instances, they see the judgments of the business offices as simply wrongheaded in regard to the gross popularity sought. In both cases, they quite correctly see their careers as contingent on the most perfect expression possible of their ideas; to consign themselves to hackdom eventually will hurt at the bank as well as before the morning mirror. The television production community is led by its distinctly different self-interest to challenge the mandate assumed by the networks. What varies is not the basis of the conflict, but its focus. At one moment, it is the advance time allowed for the production of new programming, which the entertainment makers may believe is insufficient to achieve quality; at another, it is the budgetary allowance for a particular project, which again may seem insufficient; at other times, it will be restrictions on violence or on the depiction of characters whose ethnic or religious identity may involve a risk of public objection from some organization, or a plot or treatment that may arouse controversy unredeemed by enhanced ratings.

The networks adhere to the motto of most of business: Make no enemies. This goal is expressed in the remark of one New York network executive: "Our goals will be whatever they have to be to avoid being labelled whatever the label may be." Sometimes, this desire to pare the thorns becomes piquant. When the 1979 animated version of *Flash Gordon* was in preparation for NBC, one anxious network employee looked at Ming the Merciless who rules the Planet Mongo on which Flash and his party are trapped, a figure symbolically more in tune with the days when Asia was thought of as the source of the yellow peril than the present marketing of Coca Cola in China, and said, "Can't you make him a little less yellow?" He was admirably intentioned; ethnic stereotypes need no unnecessary reinforcement. Approaches to the concoction of entertainment are illustrated as different from each other as is the philosophy of airline meal service from the cuisine of Naples.

This portrait obviously ignores many individuals. There are the consummate hacks whose clacking typewriters have never had their rhythm altered by a twinge of aesthetic ambition. There are the unabashed manipulators who think that the shriek of a housewife drowned by the shriek of an audience is about all that's happened since the Renaissance. The purity of these parties, devoid as they are of any conflict over their role as confectioners, is matched by those few in the business offices who at every opportunity will place profit secondary to other goals. The business offices are not without their visionaries. Here we encounter one of the paradoxes of television. Those who make television can more readily shed their conflicting values than those who govern it. They are more likely to be troubled, and to find their troubles deeper, because what they do is suspended between art and commerce. And although they are likely to have chosen to earn their livelihood as they do because of a nagging stake in the former, for any particular job, project, or time period they can usually surrender at least temporarily to the latter on its own terms. This is not so for those who govern, for their commanding position and the perspective on television that their role imposes dictate some concern with the public good.

What the business people and the creative people—to put the distinction in the terms employed by the two groups themselves—share, in addition to points of contention and lives beset by internal conflict, is participation in a heated, tumultuous enterprise centered in two great cities. Broadcasting as a whole is spread across the land, and its diverse elements come together annually like those of many American institutions in such centers of planned conviviality as Las Vegas; but manufacture and dissemination of the production, as contrasted with its relay to the home, are the province of New York and Los Angeles. Television people are not simply intelligent, educated, literate, verbal, and middle or upper-middle class. They are not simply cosmopolitan in looking toward colleagues for guidance and taking their cues and attaching importance to what happens thousands of miles away. They are an elite group, of course, but in particular an elite itself part of the two cultural capitals toward which the rest of the country occasionally stares and to which members of other elites who are else-where continually give their attention. New York has always been our capital of clandestine innovation in personal behavior and our display case for public experimentation in letters and the arts. Los Angeles, with its balmy but now polluted skies, beach frontage, and Mediterranean climate, has long been the circus for the open display of behavior that would be thought quirky (if not immoral) in Des Moines. Los Angeles, along with San Francisco, is where people travel to see if desperation is justified—the last chance. Its abysmal flatlands in summer stretching endlessly under yellow skies, its cheery hills and canyons bearing houses precarious before fire and landslide, the blue Pacific whose beaches draw alike the bonfires of dropouts and the homes of the professionally superordinate, are tied together by the freeways and the automobile. The English architectural writer Reyner Banham depicts the authentic L.A. in defining it as three natural ecologies—hills, seashore, and basin—united by the manmade one of concrete and Detroit or foreign sheet metal. Los Angeles is a city of distances, and the constant movement in the isolation of private vehicles from dwelling to shopping center to workplace turns people inward just as it inevitably isolates them from others. New York, by contrast, is close, crowded; its private acts necessarily shuttered to the proximity of so many eyes. New York is a convergence of elites—fashion, finance, com-munications, the great corporations, and embodies as well as it can a place of eight million, with districts so turned to rubble by poverty that war-torn is truly the right term, the traditions of achievement and excel-lence. Los Angeles, as filled with as competitive, ruthless, hard-working a citizenry as any modern city in the world, nevertheless stands for the belief that there must be more to life. It is all right to cast aside values in behalf of feeling better in L.A. The offbeat, the odd, the deviant, may come out of the closet and into the streets in New York, but they are likely to remain judged as just that and to remain isolated; in Los Angeles, they are likely to become marketed as a religion, a lifestyle, a therapy, a path of greater conformity to human potential, or a Hot Tub. Los Angeles is the capital of the conversion of personal vision to com-merce; pleasure and profit there, as in the rest of California, supposedly are easily joined.

One could speculate endlessly on the extent to which behavior and ideas openly displayed in southern California first migrated under cloak from the northeast. Certainly it would be wrong to think of Los Angeles as the id and New York the ego; the one the source of thrust and power, the other of control and sublimation. These dynamics occur within each but in each find their expression in different form. Influence shuttles back and forth and outward to the rest of the country, with the most frequently visible route exportation from California by way of New York.

Fiction gives an acutely sharp sense of the perspective shared by media people in these two cities. Writers, by trade and inclination, are close to the mass media even when ideologically antagonistic toward or professionally remote from them. Frequently, to some degree, they are or have been in their employ. They are also likely to have been or to become, willingly or churlishly, their subject. Their friends, wives, husbands, and lovers are likely to work in advertising, broadcasting, journalism, or publishing. They share with people in the media the attachment to words and the manipulation of ideas. That this is the case is exemplified by the reality of the stereotype of the advertising man with a manuscript in his drawer; Joseph Heller was one. Media people, writers themselves or not, are likely to have that vulnerability of living by other people's words. As a class, they are among that small portion of the public that reads regularly and sometimes avidly—people for whom, as Woody Allen said about himself, reading is not recreation but necessity. Novels and stories not only reflect sensibilities very often in close affinity to those of people in the media, but they are also sources by which such people shape and confirm their impressions.

For these quite apparent reasons, when we see a way of life through fiction we are often seeing it as perceived by the men and women who are responsible for television. This applies not only to places where television is given its particular character, but to the media themselves. New York is a narcissistic literary town lovingly embracing its writers and what they have written about it. Los Angeles is a closet literary town. Because of the movies, it has always been a writer's town, yet as a point of public pride or conscious recognition by its citizenry, writing is treated like sinning devoid of prurient appeal. Musso and Frank's, where Faulkner, O'Hara, and Fitzgerald drank and courted, is its sole literary shrine and the flannel cakes do not take second place. Henry James on Washington Square, Jack Kerouac and William Burroughs at the West End Cafe—there are hardly plaques enough to go around. Two very different cultures emerge from the novels and stories set in these cities. Los Angeles can be grasped, if ever so uneasily, in the barrenness of Joan Didion's *Play It As It Lays*, the defeated aspirations in the novels of Raymond Chandler, the doomed grasping at paradise in James M. Cain's *The Postman Always Rings Twice*, and the temptation to shun the obligations of the past on which turn the works of Ross MacDonald. The message of the L.A. novel is that there is something about the place that seduces and betrays. Its most perfect expression is Alison Lurie's *The Nowhere City* in which L.A. functions as a character paring a couple to their true selves, leaving the woman smugly sensual and the husband unable to hide from his need for protective conventions. New York writing charts the clash of social classes, and the manners and strategies by which people define for themselves a defendable position. Even William Gaddis' *The Recognitions*, on the surface a tale of obsession and neurosis, at root continues the lineage of Edith Wharton by chronicling how in this city deception and disguise have become the prevalent means of survival. L.A. fiction centers on the psyche and its inability out West, despite the illusion to the contrary, to escape itself or control what it will become. New York fiction centers on the struggle for dominance between the old and the new.

New York and Los Angeles in our national consciousness are both myth and promise—of excitement, the big time, success, and personal fulfillment. Yet they have evolved in that consciousness as fundamentally different, and this difference is exemplified in literature, art, and entertainment. The depictions of New York are rooted in realism and seldom transcend it. Those of Los Angeles often pass quickly from realism to caricature, and its natural end becomes a conflagration such as concludes Nathanael West's *The Day of the Locust*: the great earthquake whose destructiveness is foreshadowed in the mural on an L.A. wall of an elevated freeway crumbling into a dead end in midair. And thus there is also more than a hint in our national consciousness of an ambivalence over the reward for flight, self-indulgence, and the pursuit of pleasure.

Fiction about the media is written by people intensely close to their subject, and the Hollywood novel, the Madison Avenue novel, and the television novel are reports from the field by combatants. They bear the indelible mark of the cities in which they are set, but on some points it is fair to speak of them as one. What they tell us is what the media mean to those who work in them. The persistent theme is corrupting influence. Elizabeth Hardwick has a phrase in *Sleepless Nights*, the conversion of art to employment. What happens in mass media novels, typically, is that good intentions have unsatisfying consequences, and the causes of unrealized aspirations are the values that the media exemplify. The consuming necessity of popularity checkmates subtlety while the filtering of decisions through a bureaucracy works against originality. What is lost is the capacity of work to reflect individuality. Because the point at issue is the integrity of communication, the values that mass media are principally said to corrupt are those about communication itself. There is almost invariably a loss of innocence, sometimes over ideals but more often over the inability to maintain established standards against new criteria seemingly imposed by the marketplace. The artistic impulse, and its necessary discipline, are made secondary to the narrower but less demanding norms of professionalism; professionalism that values individual creativity gives way before the mechanistic application of audience research and committee decision-making. The television novel naturally gives particular emphasis to a second theme—the consequences of the power that accompanies prominence in the media; naturally, because television is the medium that most quickly and assuredly can elevate a performer or public figure. The message here is that of Lord Acton: Such power is so great that it defies being used well. A third common theme is that of chicanery. The media are not only portrayed as manipulative of the public, but rising within them as a matter of deceiving others. What sets the media novels apart from those about any big organization, or the New York thread merchant tales of Jerome Weidmen (*I Can Get It for You Wholesale*), is the cynicism; Sammy Glick was never a happy man, and living by the lie cost him much but not success. The fourth frequent theme is the capacity of the media to alter what people might otherwise perceive. Gavin Lambert delicately acknowledges this power in *Slide Area*, an episode in which sound effects and sensory stimuli are enough to make a blind and dying woman believe that her last days are being expended touring the sites of youthful triumph. We have seen how news on television may convey something different from the events themselves; the medium of most perfect observation is no less distorting than any other. In *The Origin of the Brunists*, Robert Coover depicts reportage of a religious cult as responsible for heightened proselytization about doomsday, and ensuing coverage as transforming the cult into a worldwide religion. When the failure of the initial prophecy is reported in the press, the members seek to vindicate themselves by gaining new adherents, and the story the media then concoct achieves legitimacy for their theorems. In each of these varied instances, reality has been reconstrued by the media.

What is one to make of such an unflattering portrait? A stranger to our culture might conclude that it expresses the views of a camp antithetical in every way to the mass media. This is undoubtedly so in certain cases, but the truth on the whole is much more paradoxical. What these novels express is recognition of the power of the economic and social machinery of the media to govern the lives of those who work within them, coupled with respect for the power of the media to influence events and public behavior and unabashed fascination with both. And there is the answer. The media for many are irresistible as places to work just because they are so powerful; the first kind of power is the test of personal worth, the second the reward, as heady as being enrobed in gold in those rare instances when no or little quarter is given in the first.

Two cities. Individuals in conflict. The division of labor between selling and making. Their establishment in our society's two symbolic capitals. A professional class, as are other professional classes, distinctly set apart from the mainstream in ways particular to itself. Ambivalence over the institution and the work that it demands. These constitute the milieu of television and the context in which its entertainment is manufactured. The strains show continually in the product in the compromises between and occasional undiluted victories of institution and individual.

There is a further way in which television entertainment is marked by its emergence from New York and Los Angeles. These two cities, in their different ways, exemplify urban culture in the United States. They constitute the frontier in thought and behavior. Media people not only constitute a distinct professional class, but the places from which they perceive the world constitute an experience distinct from that of the rest of America. Television entertainment consistently and inevitably treats topics central to life—sexual mores; crime and justice; retribution; achievement; and the use of authority men and women hold by virtue of wealth, education, and position. Although television unmistakably operates within the various confines of mass entertainment, by its very nature as a creature of these two cities invariably for many it is occasionally disturbing, at variance with values, offensive, and novel. It is a force for what sometimes may be progress and most certainly is change. The content is specifically American, but this urbanization of culture through the mass media is a phenomenon common to all societies because the media invariably emanate principally from cultural and political capitals. It is a phenomenon greatly escalated by television, for it is the medium that most closely approximates one voice rather than many in addressing a country.

PROGRAMMING

The messages of television entertainment have fascinated scholars and critics of the medium for years. The first studies focused on violence. Later studies have examined such varied topics as the portrayal of ethnic minorities, women, social class, means of personal achievement, and environmental issues. Violence, because of concern over its possible influence on the behavior of viewers, has remained a focus. These empirical examinations document the generalities of television entertainment, yet they never tell the whole story, for subtlety and exception escape them.

Television is in the business of attracting attention and sexual and moral titillation are means that are reliable. Language and behavior that come close to offending some may coincide with the social and artistic goals of the people who make television, but they also serve the medium by drawing an audience. Television is in competition with other media for disposable time in America, and a consequence is that it strives never to be dull. Much of what is on television today would not have been considered acceptable by broadcasters 15 years ago. Public tastes and social standards have changed, and television has made some contribution to these changes by probing the borders of convention accompanying each season. An image of American life flows out from Los Angeles and New York that is compatible with the urban experience peculiar to them, but for much of the country this image gently readjusts norms. For a large segment of the public, television is a follower and not a leader of social experience, but for another large segment it is a leader. It was once possible for a child to grow up unaware of homosexuality. Television has made that impossible, and has removed much of the power of the family, church, and community as guardians of knowledge. At the same time, television cannot transgress public standards to a degree that would turn audiences away, stimulate demands for increased governmental interference, or conflict with the mercenary goals of advertisers, for that would interfere with the orderly and profitable conduct of business. Thus, television weaves its occasional flirtation with nonconformity into a continuing romance with conventionality.

A pervasive theme of television entertainment is the glory that ensues from consumption. Materialism and personal satisfaction through purchase are not topics confined to commercials, but are prominent in the programming they accompany. The most obtrusive example are the game shows in which the lust for appliances and adult playthings becomes the vehicle for crude comedy and envious identification. The emphasis varies from straightforward competition for prizes to mockery conspired in by eager contestants. The lesson, admittedly not a false one, is that base motives are part of the human condition. Drama honors consumption variously by the frequency with which it portrays riches as the motive for dishonesty and scheming, the affluence in which so many characters luxuriate, and the houses and apartments that sometimes are so clearly beyond the means of those portrayed. The person we would often most like to meet is the rental agent. Occasionally, the message is startlingly explicit. In the technically superb animated special of 1978, *The Grinch Who Stole Christmas*, love for one another is not only placed at the heart of happiness, but love of new toys is placed at the heart of Christmas.

A less easy theme is that the world is a mean and risky place. The compatibility of violence and crime with the need to tell exciting stories succinctly in visual terms has made physical transgression a continuing component of television. The continuing analysis of television violence over the past decade by George Gerbner and Larry Gross at the University of Pennsylvania has led them to calculate that the likelihood of a television character falling victim to violence is about 50 times greater than the probability for the average American adult. Because television tries to avoid unnecessary offense, the physical consequences of this violence is seldom portrayed; it is quick and antiseptic. Television has been under varying intensity of attack since the early 1950s for the prevalence of violence in its entertainment, but it has been resistant and slow to change because violence has been so efficient for the hurried manufacture of tales that will attract viewers.

Television is somewhat schizophrenic in its treatment of the social hierarchy and those in positions of authority and eminence. Since the 1950s, it has depicted a world in which the social pyramid is reversed, with more people in the professional and educated middle and upper-middle classes than in the working, blue-collar, or poverty classes. Women generally defer to men and have been portrayed as subsidiary helpmates; mothers; creatures seeking status, advantageous marriage, or sexual liaison; or objects of sexual conquest. The subordination of women in daytime and primetime drama has been reinforced by their portrayal in the accompanying commercials. When two social psychologists, Leslie McArthur and Beth Resko, examined the frequency with which men and women were depicted as users and experts in about 200 commercials in 1971 for home, food, and body products, they found that men were overwhelmingly presented as having expertise about these products, although for each commercial women were presented as constituting the majority of users. The disparity was most extreme for home products, where women made up about 85 percent of users but men made up about 85 percent of those displaying authoritative knowledge. In drama, men, usually white, almost invariably youthful or in the prime of life, sometimes prosperous members of a profession such as law or medicine but often ambiguous as to the source of their very apparent means, are generally the fulcrums of decision and action. Women in television drama have entered the labor force at a much slower rate than in real life. Minorities were infrequently seen before an explicit change in network policy in the late 1960s, and since then they have consistently constituted slightly more than 10 percent of all characters. By honoring what admittedly has been our society's actual pecking order, television has been a force in maintaining it. On the other hand, the proclivity of television drama for confrontations between powerful forces of good and evil has led to the frequent portrayal of men of considerable stature as conniving and dishonest. Businessmen cheat, embezzle, murder to advance themselves, and torch their factories to collect the insurance. Politicians conspire to preclude the disclosure of iniquity. Doctors and psychiatrists are an exception: They not only escape calumny, but are typically portrayed as extraordinarily effective. Television minimizes risk, and the helping professions in our culture, besides having organizations quick to flare at public taint, are sacrosanct from interference in their effectiveness—with the result that a question rarely raised in drama is the wisdom of seeking their aid. Television in this particular instance reinforces public dependence on those with degrees, certification, and an elaborate education whose business is the vending of expertise. By attributing such behavior to those in positions of responsibility, television undermines faith in many institutions while reinforcing the status of a few.

Television is similarly schizophrenic in its treatment of law enforcement. Police and private detectives solve crimes with a success rate matched in actual practice only by the ticketing of parking violators by meter maids. Private eyes in real life seldom are central to a criminal investigation, but in television drama the miscarriage of justice is often only averted by their intervention. It is one of the ironies of television that while criminals sometimes admit to learning useful techniques and dodges from television, police officials almost invariably find television drama at sharp variance with real police work. Television certainly does insist that crime does not pay, but it also often implies that the law must be broken in order to bring criminals to justice. Lawyers have tallied numerous instances in television drama in which arrest and conviction have hinged on the abrogation of Constitutional guarantees. *Dirty Harry* is a stock figment of television. A hero commands the attention of the audience by rising above circumstances, so the decisive step that violates normal procedure is a common device of television drama. When sociologist Otto Larsen and his colleagues examined the goals and means of their achievement in network drama years ago, they found that stratagems antisocial by being either illegal or employing violence constituted more than a third of the means used to achieve goals that in themselves were socially approved. On television, justice and law are not synonymous.

Belief in the occult, life on other planets, life after death, and hidden and possibly malevolent purpose behind the inexplicable, subjects so relentlessly exploited by the tabloids aimed at the lip-reading public that enliven passage through the check-out counter, have not been ignored by television. In comedy and drama, for general audiences as well as for children, humans with supernatural powers, beings from outer space, witches, ghosts, and vampires have been frequent. Documentary cameras have focused on the empty field where some strange residue was said to mark the landing of a flying saucer. Perhaps there are things about which our scientific age knows not enough, or at least no more than its self-confidence could bear. Television's parade of little green men, like its procession of western and urban lawmen, is intended to divert and excite, but it also preys on doubts about the natural order of the universe, hopes for immortality, superstition, and ignorance. Superficially harmless, catering to the public's interest in such topics reinforces beliefs that there are those among us who are more or less than human, that there are dark and ominous forces at work, that rationality may be an untrustworthy guide, and that a select few are in closer communication with the powers of the universe. In so doing, such entertainment implies that most of us are woefully weak and at the mercy of influences beyond reason or our control. Thus, this superficially harmless diversion transforms the occult into a rationale for submission to the totalitarianism of the cult.

Life is not only predatory on television, but it is also beset by troubles. The daytime soap operas portray life as a succession of crises carrying people first closer to, then drawing them away from, a stylish liaison, an object of ardor, wealth, or possible harm. The soap opera is the Grand Hotel formula at the community level. A handful of characters, each pursuing an independent destiny, variously become entangled in each others' lives. Each lifeline is a series of trials and mishaps—marital infidelity, psychosomatic illness, bigamy, alcoholism, drug abuse, a failing business, a dishonored promise. Everything is ultimately quite hopeless because the troubles keep on coming, but the characters ceaselessly struggle against the tide. These tribulations are distinct from the conflicts that are central to primetime drama by representing nothing more than the dark underside of humdrum life, as if the pathetic trivia from the inside of newspapers must also find its place on television. The audience looks upward much of the time in these stories, for they are tales heavily populated by the middle and upper-middle classes and particularly professionals. If the problems are unusual in quantity and regularity, they are less so in degree and not at all in category—drugs, booze, sex, marriage, money worries. The stories illustrate modes of coping, and emphasize the seeking of professional help. The soap operas thus provide some solace by depicting the troubles of others as more oppressive if similar, with help or resolution possible; the largely female audience can identify with little or no discomfort.

Self-interest is what gives shape to what is broadcast, and the way conventionality is the invariable framework in soap opera and primetime programming for selected deviation exemplifies this principle. In soap opera, abortion is seldom treated as acceptable. Premarital cohabitation, divorce, and illegitimacy are portrayed as facts of life. The distinction is between an action that would arouse the partisanship of viewers and religious orders, and statuses that have come to be accepted as perhaps troublesome or regrettable but beyond condemnation. During primetime, homosexuality and racial antagonism can be placed in comedy more easily than in drama because the former permits ambiguity in regard to approval. The increased proportion of black and other ethnic minority characters during the past decade has enjoyed the same inverse social structure as have whites, with more in the middle and upper-middle classes than in lower strata—although in real life the pyramid is more sharply exaggerated for these groups. The caution with which television enters new territory is illustrated by the tendency for blacks, when they began to appear more frequently in commercials a decade ago, to be placed in larger-than-ordinary crowds of whites to ensure that they would be unobtrusive.

Nowhere is this invisible hand of prudence more strikingly displayed than in the treatment of the environment in comedy and drama in the early 1970s. Rutgers historian Richard Heffner and his colleague Esther Kramer found that during a week of network programming topics were treated in accord with their potential for disrupting television's orderly conduct of business. Conservation and nature were treated approvingly and pollution was condemned, in line with public sympathies. Population control, although opportunities occurred for favorable or unfavorable treatment, was dealt with obliquely and ambiguously. Where television had a direct interest through its advertising revenues, in transportation, private means were strongly favored over public means. Television drama and comedy take their risks with calculation.

Love and kindness have not been predominant in television drama, although certainly passion and sexual desire have had a prominent place. The need for conflict and striving as narrative devices have relegated certain of the more positive, supportive aspects of human interaction to a secondary place. There have been numerous noteworthy exceptions, such as *The Waltons*, *Little House on the Prairie*, and many dramas outside the series format, but on the whole the more brittle, abrasive, and manipulatory aspects of human relations have been emphasized. Situation comedies, from *The Adventures of Ozzie and Harriet* and *Father Knows Best* to the more acidic *All in the Family*, have frequently revolved around the warmth of family life, although they often have been sappy at best and at worst have presented their viewers with a household so elevated economically and emotionally from reality that the contrast at times could only be disheartening. Sexual yearning in comedy naturally has usually been a source of embarrassment or a matter for mockery; in drama, it has been confined largely to a source of gratification, a motive for antisocial behavior, or a drive that leads to peril. It is seldom treated as something fundamentally constructive or often problematical. There is certainly little of the attachment that psychoanalysis has made so prominent in western thought (and Norman Mailer in his fiction) of sexual drive to creativity and violence—unless one is willing to accept the standards of guilt by association. Television seldom presents parents, particularly both mother and father, in any kind of loving relationship with small children. The family warmth on television has been largely confined to broken homes, families with adolescents, or relationships between parents and their grown children. It is not that television's portrayal of human relationships is inaccurate in the particular; rather, it is selective and by telling only part of the story distorts the whole. The barriers, again, are television's allegiance to conventionality—in this case, certain admittedly established conventions of popular entertainment, and the quite possibly correct assumption on the part of most of those who sell television and many of those who make television that the examined life has dubious value as a means of assembling audiences in behalf of profits.

These conventions of popular entertainment provide television, as they do other media, with rules that minimize the possibility of public offense. Explicit violence is acceptable; explicit sex, less so. Sexual behavior is most acceptable when treated as a device to facilitate narrative or comedy. Crime cannot pay, but justice vindicates violence and violation of the law. By adhering to such rules—which, of course, are often violated in the cause of artistic or mercenary motives—the media escape criticism. Television is particularly conformist because it enters the home and seeks to satisfy at every moment a huge and heterogeneous audience. On television, the idealized escapades of solitary men and, less frequently, women and the elevated social milieus provide objects of admiration and a vicarious upward mobility. Retribution, so often inadvisable in real life, can be enjoyed indirectly. The trappings of a better life so continually displayed do not become oppressive because they are mitigated by demonstrations that affluence does not bring happiness. Such entertainment is escapist in the sense of partially evading reality, but is not without its positive contributions. Harold Mendelsohn, in *Mass Entertainment*, argued many years ago that it is redeemed by the pleasure it brings to millions in transporting them from their daily lives and preaching messages they find satisfying. Superficiality, he said, was the price that had to be paid. It would be silly not to recognize that television brings pleasure and that is valuable, but it is not a corollary that the means are invariably beneficial or that it should not be expected to do more.

These many and varied themes are interspersed with continuing illustrations of exemplary behavior. Daring rescues, selflessness, and the struggle against difficult odds have accompanied the conflict and violence in nighttime drama. Eliot Ness of *The Untouchables* was a cold fish, *Kojak* suppressed his sympathy for human frailty, and *Starsky and Hutch* have never been long on empathy or police procedure, but they cannot be faulted for persistence, immunity to temptation, or bravery. Compassion characterized the protagonists of such long-running action series as *Naked City* and *Route 66*. Logic and the painful comprehension of human greed have been the techniques of crime solution in *Perry Mason, Colombo*, and *Barnaby Jones*. *Cannon* was too fat to substitute muscle for mind. *Gunsmoke*, the longest-running series in television history when finally canceled after 20 years in 1975, featured in Matt Dillon a lawman who was intelligent, concerned as much for the welfare of his townsfolk as for the letter of the law, and, while iron in resolve and unflinching before danger, never one to resort to violence except when it was his only recourse. The father-and-son lawyer team of *The Defenders* scrupulously weighed questions of morality and ethics while seeking justice for their clients under the law. In *The Avengers* and *Policewoman,* as well as in such situation comedies as *The Mary Tyler Moore Show* and *Maude,* women have been portrayed as capable, resourceful humans able to lead as well as follow—a characterization that also can hardly be denied to the plastic cyberneticism of *The Bionic Woman. The Mod Squad* made cooperation among races and the sexes a central element of plot, and portrayed teenagers as responsible young adults instead of butts of laughter or problems for society. *Barney Miller* found comedy in the station house, but its mockery is generally so gentle and so confounded with the portrayal of admirable human qualities that it evokes empathy. The daytime serials, although darkly oneiric by the choking difficulty they attribute to life, do present some people who attempt to solve their problems rationally, and few who could be said to surrender easily. Television regularly portrays human endeavor at its peak or at its best; its conventions and the conventionality of treatment these foster simply do not lead to its full portrayal.

VIEWER PSYCHOLOGY

The psychology of how the messages (inevitably a part of entertainment) instruct viewers has not been exhaustively explored, but a number of principles have been established by empirical investigation. Two leaders in this endeavor have been the well-known psychologists Albert Bandura and Leonard Berkowtiz. The means they and their followers have employed have been a series of intriguing laboratory-type experiments that meet rigorous scientific standards.

These investigations have focused largely, but not exclusively, on the influence of violent film and television portrayals on the subsequent behavior of viewers, and there are many important differences that set apart the studies associated with the two men. What they have in common is a concern for the underlying mental processes on which any learning that transpires from viewing television is contingent.

The experiments conducted by Bandura have used children of nursery school age as subjects. Obviously, the results apply most clearly at this age, but they also have relevance in regard to adults and older children. There are two reasons for their broad generalizability, both related to the way science proceeds. Young children in this case were simply the best subjects for testing propositions about the influence of television because their relatively undeveloped repertoires of behavior made it more likely that some link could be readily demonstrated between what was seen and what later was done, and the purpose of the scientific experiment is to examine relationships between cause and effect under optimally sensitive conditions. The experiments also have a claim to wide applicability because they are derived from a formulation called social learning theory that offers a very convincing explanation for much of human behavior. Thus, children are not the limit on but the means to general knowledge.

The framework for these experiments has been much the same as that of the first one published in the *Journal of Abnormal and Social Psychology* in 1963. The subjects were about 100 nursery school boys and girls divided into four groups, each of which then had a very different experience. One group saw an adult attack a Bobo doll—a large, inflated balloon figure—in a number of specific ways accompanied by such declarations of wrath as "Sock him in the nose! Kick Him!" In a second, they saw the identical attack in a color film portrayal shown on a television receiver. In a third, they saw the identical attack via color television carried out by a woman dressed as Cat Lady, the type of fantasy personage that appears in children's programming. And in a fourth, the control condition, they saw no attacks. Afterward, each child was given the opportunity to play for 20 minutes while being observed through two-way mirrors. To enhance their inclination to behave aggressively, the children were mildly frustrated by being led away from a room full of attractive toys to the relatively more barren second play area. In this new situation, there was a Bobo doll; a mallet such as the one employed in the assault; other items conducive to aggressive play, such as dart guns and a tether ball with a painted face hanging from the ceiling; and an assortment of toys unassociated with aggression, such as a tea set, cars and trucks, and crayons and coloring paper.

The children who had seen an example of violence were themselves more aggressive in their play. In each of the three conditions in which there was a display of aggression, between 80 and 90 percent of the children duplicated one or more acts they had seen performed. The children exposed to violence also exceeded those in the control condition in quantity of aggressive play different from what had been seen. Those who had seen the live demonstration displayed more aggressive behavior than those who had seen the Cat Lady television sequence, but both the Cat Lady and the human portrayals were followed by greater aggressiveness than occurred in the control condition.

The increase in aggressiveness different from the demonstrations could have resulted from the excitement produced by the experience, but the greater quantity of duplicative behavior means that the varied exposures to violent behavior provided examples, or lessons, that were followed. Observing what adults in real life and on television did changed what the children chose to do when confronted with stimuli from the adult environment. Observation can be thought of as adding to the repertoire of behavior of which the children were capable, or of changing the meaning of the stimuli and thereby the behavior that was displayed when they were encountered. The fact that the Cat Lady television sequence had less effect than the live demonstration suggests that cues encouraging the interpretation of observed behavior as make-believe or fantasy reduces its instructional efficacy, but the fact that both television versions had some effect implies that experiencing something through an audiovisual medium has an impact similar in kind to direct, real-life experience. This is precisely what those imbued with the power of television have been saying for years: It duplicates distant reality in the livingroom.

This experiment followed one published two years earlier that had demonstrated that children would learn simply by observing others, without practice or direct reinforcement of the act in question, but it extended the principle to vicarious, televised, or filmed experience. The first step was the demonstration of the basic psychological process; the second, of its applicability to television and film. Soon after, there began to appear in scientific journals experiments exploring the conditions upon which such instructional effects are contingent.

The next experiment by Bandura belongs to this strand. In the control condition, no televised films were seen. In the three other conditions, nursery school boys and girls saw a color television sequence in which either two adults named Rocky and Johnny played vigorously with several balls, a Bobo doll, a hula hoop, a lasso, dart guns, a baton, cars, and plastic farm animals; Rocky attacked Johnny, gained control of the toys, and received 7-Up and cookies; or Rocky attacked Johnny, but was successfully repulsed by Johnny. In each case, Rocky displayed a number of discrete, identifiable aggressive acts in playing with the toys. In the version in which Rocky is victorious, Rocky attacks after he is refused access to the toys, stumbles, and is pounced on by Johnny but thoroughly defeats him, and after eating the cookies and drinking the 7-Up leaves the scene with the toys packed in a bag singing, "Hi ho, hi ho, it's off to play I go" while Johnny cowers in a corner. Events are the same in the sequence in which Rocky is defeated, except roles are reversed and it is Rocky who is shown cowering in the corner.

Subsequently, in the playroom, the children who saw Rocky apparently rewarded for his behavior emulated his aggressive play. Those who saw him punished or not rewarded did not emulate him. In later interviews, those who saw Rocky as victorious were highly critical of him but expressed the desire to behave like him—an inclination that they had fulfilled in their actual behavior—and they made derogatory remarks about his victim. Those who saw Rocky punished were also critical of him, but did not make derogatory remarks about Johnny. The results validate the intuitive judgment that children do not think much of a loser. The larger implica-

Experiments

tion is that television portrayals are most efficacious as instruction when behavior is depicted as successful or rewarded.

The experiments of Berkowitz and his followers, which also began to appear in 1963, further elaborate some of the means by which television instructs its audience. In these experiments, the subjects were of college age, so the results are most clearly relevant to young adults. However, they also elucidate general principles that would appear to apply much more widely.

The paradigm is the same for a number of experiments. Subjects are first frustrated, subsequently undergo vicarious experience by seeing one or another film, then have the opportunity to behave aggressively against their frustrator. What varies principally among them is the content of the films, and what they have in common is that differences in the behavior of the subjects appear to be the consequence of the instruction the films have conveyed.

The first experiment, published in the *Journal of Abnormal and Social Psychology*, is typical. It addressed the question of whether vicarious exposure to violence by film or television reduces aggressive drive, thereby lessening the likelihood of aggressive behavior. This is the catharsis hypothesis which holds that exposure to a violent portrayal purges viewers of aggressive inclinations. Earlier, another psychologist, Seymour Feshbach, had published an experiment in which angered subjects had displayed less subsequent aggressive imagery in response to a word test after viewing a violent film, which seemed to support such a proposition. Berkowitz thought otherwise. He acknowledged the legitimacy of the results, but not the validity of the interpretation. He argued that the psychological dynamic involved was not catharsis, but inhibition. He reasoned that the film had sensitized the subjects to their aggressive impulses, much as a pornographic film might sensitize viewers to double entendre or sexual motives, and that they had curbed its symbolic expression.

In order to test his interpretation, Berkowitz designed an experiment in which the likelihood of inhibition would be minimized in one condition. If catharsis were responsible for the earlier outcome, then aggression in such a circumstance also would be reduced. If, however, aggression was greater when inhibitory factors were minimized, catharsis could not be claimed as the dynamic at work. The subjects were first insulted and harassed during an I.Q. test by the experimenter's assistant. After viewing the films, their tasks included rating the professional proficiency of the assistant in a manner that implied the ratings could affect his career. Inhibitory tendencies were thus reduced by providing a target who could be thought of as deserving retribution. The film sequence was the brutal prize fight from the Kirk Douglas movie *Champion* (United Artists, 1949). The principal comparison involved a condition in which the beating administered to Douglas was described as the just reward of a scoundrel and another in which Douglas was said to be a good man beginning to show remorse for his misdeeds. In the jargon of psychology, this pitted a portrayal of justified aggression against a portrayal of unjustified aggression. The catharsis hypothesis would predict similarly reduced hostility in both conditions as the consequence of the vicarious experience of violence. In fact, the subjects displayed greater unfavorability (or more hostility) in their ratings after viewing the justified aggression. The combination of a deserving target and filmed illustration of revenge overcame inhibitions about aggressive impulses aroused by the vicarious experience. The implication is that these subjects took what they had seen as an example of appropriate behavior and applied it to their own circumstances.

In later, similar experiments, other ways in which films—and presumably television—can alter behavior were explored. In one, the name of the experimental target of aggression was varied. In one condition, he was identified as Bob; in another, as Kirk, the same name as the film victim. In these later experiments, irritation of the subjects was achieved by someone administering mild electric shocks as feedback on a task, and aggression after viewing was measured by the electric shocks delivered by the subjects as feedback to this same person in a like task. This aversive experience was necessary to ensure some degree of aggressive drive directed toward the target that could be subject to media influence. In this instance, aggression was greater when the name of the target matched that of the film victim. Seeing the film either lowered inhibitions or stimulated aggression when the recipient of the shocks was named Kirk. The implication is that the film altered the meaning of the environmental cue of the target's name.

In several experiments, the meaning that is attributed by a viewer to a portrayal has been demonstrated to affect subsequent behavior. In one instance, college-age subjects who saw a film of a football game whose participants were described as intent on injuring each other subsequently delivered a greater degree of electric shocks than those who saw the same athletic encounters when they were said to involve athletes engaging in their profession. In two other instances, college-age subjects who viewed the fight sequence from *Champion* displayed greater aggressiveness, again measured by electric shock delivery, when the boxers were described as vengeful than when they were said to be cool professionals. In television entertainment, the plot guides viewer interpretation. What these experiments suggest is that an example of malicious or retributive behavior in television drama at least temporarily alters the viewer's judgment about how to act.

In several other experiments, the behavior of subjects has been affected by the description of a television or film portrayal as accurately representing real events instead of being a fictional account. In one, a war sequence was described as a realistic account for some college-age subjects and a fictional account for others. In another, college-age subjects were either told that a videotape of men fighting in a parking lot was real or a staged affray. In a third, children of elementary school age were either told that a film of college rioting was newsreel footage or clips from a Hollywood drama. In the first two, the subjects delivered a greater degree of electric shocks when the war sequence was described as realistic; in the third, the children delivered a higher level of aversive noise when told the rioting had actually occurred. Television drama by definition is fictional, but like all fiction it often claims public attention by its ostensible reflection of reality. In these experiments, the belief that the behavior observed was true to life apparently enhanced the likelihood of it serving as a model for the viewer's own behavior.

When viewers identify with a character they are more likely to experience the portrayal as instructive. Male subjects of elementary school age saw a film of a boy playing a war strategy game. Some were told that, according to a questionnaire they had completed, the boy in the film was very similar to themselves in interests and abilities, and others were told that he was not at all like themselves. When given an opportunity to play the same war strategy game after viewing the film, the boys who had been told they were similar to the boy in the portrayal more frequently aped his strategy. The implication is that television entertainment is particularly likely to function as instruction when persons portrayed are perceived by viewers as somehow similar to themselves—a circumstance certainly achieved at many points in television drama.

The interpretation that viewers give to what they see on the screen is obviously governed not only by the plot but by their own experience, as this experiment demonstrates. For example, in another experiment, college-age subjects delivered a lesser degree of electric shocks after hearing censorious remarks about the behavior portrayed in a violent sequence from the James Dean movie *Rebel Without a Cause* (Warner Brothers, 1955) than when they did not hear such remarks. The instructive potential of entertainment depends partly on the presence or absence of an explicit judgment about the desirability of the behavior in question—a judgment that television drama often delivers itself through the reactions and comments of its characters.

There is a formulation in psychology developed by Percy Tannenbaum and Dolf Zillmann which holds that behavioral effects attributable to the viewing of a film or television episode may result from the excitement induced by the experience. This is the arousal hypothesis, and it predicts that any stirring exposure to these media heightens the likelihood of whatever behavior is subsequently appropriate. Its validity is demonstrated by an experiment conducted by Zillmann in which college-age subjects were exposed either to a violent film, an erotic film, or an uncompelling and bland film. As in the Berkowitz experiments, the subjects first received mild electric shocks, saw one or another of the films, then had the opportunity to deliver shocks to the person from whom they had earlier received shocks. Subjects who had seen the violent and erotic films delivered a greater degree of shock; those who had seen the erotic film delivered a greater degree of shock than those who had seen the violent film. Other experiments have confirmed that exciting portrayals can alter the viewer's state of arousal. Blood pressure, sweating, skin resistance, and other measures of physiological arousal have been heightened demonstrably by exposure to such portrayals. The psychologist Russell Geen, for example, found that the observation of a videotape of a supposedly real fight between two men maintained the level of increased blood pressure induced among college-age subjects by the receipt of electric shocks from a confederate of the experimenter, while viewing the same videotape was accompanied by a decline in blood pressure to a normal level for those either not provoked by the confederate or seeing the same combat labeled as simulated, and that sweating was increased when the fight was labeled real. As we would expect, provoked subjects were more aggressive, as measured by their delivery of electric shocks to the confederate, after viewing the portrayal said to represent a real fight.

Emotional arousal probably plays a role in the varied experimental results that have been attributed to the instructional influence of television and film. The arousal hypothesis gains credence from the fact that in many of these and other experiments, provoking subjects by the administration of electric shock by itself has been enough to increase the degree of aggressiveness displayed, for such an experience can be interpreted as another means to emotional arousal. However, there are a number of reasons why the arousal hypothesis at best is a partial explanation, and instruction merits the status of a major contributor.

First, arousal does not explain the imitative influence of portrayals. It might explain heightened levels of behavior, such as increased nonimitative aggression when it occurs in the Bandura experiments, but not behavior identical to what has been viewed. Second, arousal fails to account for certain of the observed effects, unless one is willing to engage in the nonscientific expedient of blindly inferring arousal and only arousal whenever there is a demonstrated influence on behavior. There is no sound reason for believing that rewarded, justified, or malicious violence, a portrayal in which the victim's name matches that of the real-life target, the perception of a portrayal as representing reality, or the belief that someone in a portrayal is like oneself are more arousing than a television or film sequence conveying the identical behavior under a different label or circumstances. The view that arousal is not the sole factor is supported by an ingenious analysis by two communications researchers, Robert Krull and James Watt, Jr. They correlated scores of aggressive behavior obtained from about 600 adolescents with their prior television viewing. The programs, representing a substantial quantity of viewing, were scored both for violent content and for various other features in the hands of the director that could be considered exciting, such as the pace. They found that each of these two elements, violence and the capacity to excite, were associated with greater aggressiveness on the part of the adolescents, and that the relationship occurred for each independently when the influence of the other was statistically eliminated. If arousal were the sole relevant factor, the association between violence and aggressiveness would not have survived the extraction of the exciting visual treatment by which the violence was depicted. These two researchers conclude that a program may affect behavior either through arousing the viewer or by providing information.

Nonexperimental research adds to the psychology of entertainment as instruction. Two sociologists, Melvin and Lois DeFleur, examined the impressions several hundred midwestern elementary school children had of occupations, some of which they knew about from real life, some which they could know only from television, and others which they had encountered neither in real life nor on television. They found that, for occupations outside their experience, the children knew much more about those featured on television. The DeFleurs also found that the children were more alike in the degree of prestige attributed to the occupations they had encountered only on television than for either those they knew about from real life or had not encountered at all, and these assessments of prestige were closer to those of their parents than their other assessments. The sociologists interpret this heightened consistency in response to what was portrayed on television as reflecting a homogenizing influence of the stereotypes common in mass entertainment. Another sociologist, Walter Gerson, provides similar data in his study of more than 600 black and white adolescents in San Francisco. He sought information about reliance on the mass media for norms—in particular, for guidance about how to interact with the opposite sex. He found that blacks reported using the mass media, and principally television, much more frequently than did whites both to confirm their notions about appropriate behavior and to get new dating ideas. Among the blacks, those who had found friends and a place for themselves in the miniature society of their peers were more likely to rely on the media; among the whites, those relatively excluded from peer culture more often turned to the media. Among the whites, girls were the predominant users of the media; among the blacks, boys. The explanatory factor for the whole pattern appears to be relative deprivation of information. The black teenagers would be somewhat more in doubt about the norms of the wider, predominantly white society, and those most eager for the kind of information in question would be males well enough situated to further themselves in peer society. Among the whites, such information deprivation conceivably would be most common among females, for whom available firsthand sources might prove inadequate to their levels of interest, and certainly among males cut off from peers. These two studies support the conclusion that television entertainment is instructive when it provides information not readily available firsthand, but that the information obtained from television may be narrowly restricted compared with that which real life would supply.

Joseph Klapper, in his succinct and comprehensive analysis of the scientific evidence up to 1960, *The Effects of Mass Communication,* argued that the influence of the media is largely confined to reinforcing predispositions and already present inclinations. The view that television instructs when what it conveys is novel might be taken as conflicting with such a perspective. In fact, there is no conflict. Television entertainment undoubtedly does both, and novel information would be expected to have its greatest impact when it fits existing motives and needs. The would-be criminal will find his caper, the housewife her ameliorative strategy, the adolescent the means of achieving social success.

These studies by psychologists and sociologists lead to a number of principles about television entertainment as a source of information. Television is instructive because it provides examples that people can apply to their own circumstances. These examples are particularly likely to be followed when the behavior is portrayed as efficacious or rewarding. They are also likely to be followed when the behavior is endowed with social approval—a notion that best seems to incorporate the findings about justified and malicious violence, for the common element is the message that retribution is conventional. Instruction similarly becomes more likely when what is portrayed is made particularly relevant to the viewer—for this appears to be the element uniting the findings about a cue in a portrayal that matches one in real life, the depiction of a portrayal as representing real-life events, and perceived similarity with a character in a portrayal. Instruction also becomes more likely when television presents information not available from the environment, and particularly so when that information represents something about which the viewer wants to know. What remains unclear, and what probably will never be fully untangled, is the degree to which television serves as a source of information compared with other influences. However, it so frequently exemplifies in its programming the principles on which instruction by entertainment rests that it is probable that television often instructs at least a few in the audience, and in some instances instructs many.

5

GROWING UP

Few would quarrel with the applicability to much of television of Groucho Marx's judgment in *Duck Soup* (1933), "A five-year-old child would understand this. Send someone to fetch a five-year-old child." Television, of course, does not require anyone to fetch the child. Children typically are quickly captivated by television, and view it regularly throughout their young lives. They apparently find something they can understand, and they do so at almost all hours of the broadcast schedule, for there are sizable numbers of children viewing every day from morning until as late as 10 p.m. Viewing, of course, is heaviest from midafternoon through early primetime and on Saturday and Sunday mornings, but much of what children view is intended for general audiences. What children understand of what they see is a question not answerable by inquires directed to adults, for children cannot comprehend the subtleties of plot, the motives of characters, and the consequences of action to the same degree as can adults. Yet, episodic though their appreciation may be, it is undeniably real enough at the youngest of ages and it never appreciably diminishes, although viewing in terms of hours per week changes as children grow older. Children have been the focus of numerous studies concerned with the social effects of television, and the issues addressed include the medium's influence on their behavior, the impact of its unremitting mercantile emphasis, and its role in their development toward adulthood.

EARLY AND LATE

Television in the lives of our children. That phrase perfectly expresses both the motive and scope of the skepticism, fear, and uneasy acceptance evoked by television in connection with child rearing. It very early becomes the focus of an infant's attention. It introduces the child to comedy, drama, animation, and to mass entertainment as a part of life; several hours a day from shortly after birth through the teen-age years typically are spent in the company of television, as they will continue to be during adulthood. Television is initially a pacifier upon which parents often rely, and quite soon it becomes a source of information about much that is unfamiliar and sometimes disconcerting or alarming to parents. It is quickly sought for diversion from the everyday and occasionally for escape, in the sense of immersion in a distracting distant world, from anxiety and unhappiness. The phrase is also the title of a justly famous although, by the standards of popular American publishing, obscure book by Wilbur Schramm, Jack Lyle, and Edwin Parker that has been reprinted many times since its first appearance 20 years ago. *Television in the Lives of Our Children* assessed, through the assembly of data on thousands of American children and parents, the place the then-new medium had come to occupy in the hours and minds of the young.

Like much in life, television is not quite like anything else. It is an experience paralleled only in a few ways with the experience of children prior to the middle of the twentieth century. Certainly it has taken patronage away from other media by serving many of the same social and psychological functions more conveniently, but it is also distinct even from its most obvious parallel—theater movies— by its presence in the home, the paradoxical difficulty of parental censorship, the discontinuous but continual nature of attention, the narrower norms for content dictated by pursuit of a mass audience, and the amount of time for which it accounts. Television is no more the same thing as the movies as *Don Quixote* is indistinguishable from *Doonesbury*.

The study by Schramm, Lyle, and Parker has not since been equaled in scale in the United States except by the Surgeon General's inquiry into television violence in the early 1970s. However, it was preceded by a similarly extensive investigation in England by Hilde Himmelweit, A. N. Oppenheim, and Pamela Vince (*Television and the Child*). These two enterprises, one in America and one in England, are the foundation for understanding the role of television in socialization. Although their findings have been elaborated and qualified by later research, the conclusions and interpretations of these pioneering investigators remain pertinent today.

Their perspective is accurately summarized in a statement by Schramm and colleagues so frequently quoted that only its essential truth has continued to redeem it from abandonment as a cliche:

> For *some* children under *some* conditions, some television is harmful. For *other* children under the same conditions, or for the same children under *other* conditions, it may be beneficial. For *most* children, under *most* conditions, *most* television is probably neither particularly harmful nor particularly beneficial.

The truth is that the influence of television depends on the characteristics and circumstances of the young viewer as well as on what is portrayed; the attribution of goodness or badness depends on the values introduced by the person sitting in judgment; and the vicarious experience that is television entertainment eludes any simple unidimensional evaluation. The statement should not blind us to the several issues on which many would agree that some doubt about the beneficence of the medium is justified.

Television was found to consume a sizable amount of children's time, although substantially less than what would be the case two decades later. By the late 1970s, the average time during a typical fall week recorded by the A.C. Nielsen Company for children 2-11 years of age was 28 hours, and, for teenagers 12-17, 22 hours. As with adults, the penetration of daily life by television has increased with the passage of time. Brighter children watched less, a distinction that no longer seems quite so pronounced, if it exists at all. The passage of time and the accompanying greater acceptance of the medium as part of life (instead of an enemy of print) by adults, many of whom had grown up with television, has meant more uniform, homogeneous usage relatively undifferentiated by intellectual capacity among children. Viewing was decidedly greater by children from families lower in socioeconomic status, a distinction that remains because of the greater range of alternative ways to spend time open to children of more affluent, better-educated parents. Minor vocabulary advantages soon vanished as children advanced in school; increased knowledge was largely limited to knowledge about the stars and programming of television. Then, as now, consumption of television increased through the elementary school years, then declined somewhat as children entered high school and the increased personal freedom and social involvements that it brings. Children were quite often frightened by violence in drama, but it was violence atypical of the flow of conflict that most often was disturbing— violence that flared in a familiar, usually peaceful setting, threatened a child or adult with whom they could identify, or employed a knife or other instrument from everyday life. Young viewers quickly became accustomed to the ritualized violence exemplified by the then-popular westerns.

AGGRESSIVENESS

Neither the Schramm nor Himmelweit study found any association between delinquent or aggressive behavior and television viewing, but neither focused finely on the possibility of a relationship between the viewing of violent programming and such behavior, nor did the studies offer any support for the view that such programming is cathartic or ameliorative in regard to destructive or hurtful acts. The evidence that violent programming may encourage behavior that is antisocial—in the sense of being unconducive to peaceful human interaction—began to accumulate with the 1963 experiments of Bandura and Berkowitz. By the time of the Surgeon General's inquiry at the beginning of the 1970s, about 50 experiments, in the course of developing a psychology of entertainment's behavior influence, demonstrating that children and college students were likely to display increased aggressiveness immediately after viewing a violent portrayal had been published.

The examination of television violence by the U.S. Surgeon General was undertaken at the explicit request of Senator John Pastore. His letter to the Secretary of Health, Education, and Welfare asking for a study that would "establish scientifically in so far as possible" whether violent programming contributed to antisocial behavior on the part of viewers resulted in the budgeting of $1 million for new research and the appointment of a panel of experts to evaluate the results. This group, the Surgeon General's Scientific Advisory Committee on Television and Social Behavior, was once playfully described as made up of "the network five, the naive four, and the scientific three." HEW, in one of those steps humans retrospectively describe as "it seemed a good idea at the time," solicited the three networks and the National Association of Broadcasters for persons deemed unsuitable for appointment as well as for suggestions for membership. CBS declined to offer any advice, but NBC, ABC, and the NAB named seven persons as unsuitable, presumably because of their public statements or writings on the question or because of the research they had conducted, including three very well-known behavioral scientists: Albert Bandura, Leonard Berkowitz, and Percy Tannenbaum. Ostensibly, the purpose of seeking such advice was to enhance credibility and cooperation on the part of the broadcasting business and was in accord with the procedure followed in regard to the tobacco industry in assembling the Surgeon General's panel on smoking and health—except that in that case organizations aligned on both sides of the controversy were asked to identify unsuitable parties. When the committee was finally appointed, it included five persons closely affiliated with the networks—a psychologist and a sociologist who were NBC and CBS executives, and three social scientists who consulted regularly for CBS—and four others—an anthropologist, a physician, a psychiatrist, and a professor of child development, all well known and thoroughly expert in their own fields—who were decidely unfamiliar with the empirical study of communication effects. Only three persons, two psychologists and a political scientist, could be said to be free of close affiliation with the business whose product was under scrutiny and also said to possess technical expertise. The "naive four," of course, reflected the common if not always sensible policy of hetereogeneous representation for such panels; the broadcasting representation, in many people's eyes, reflected the power of the business and the disinclination of the administration of Richard Nixon to offend it unnecessarily.

Offense to broadcasting may have been minimized, but offense to the scientific community was the price, and ironically that price has been paid by broadcasting itself. Controversy over the integrity of the committee continued for years after the revelation of the blackballing in the press, and eventually was only quieted when the group's conclusion became clearly understood as supporting the view that violent programming enhances the likelihood of aggressiveness on the part of young viewers. However, the presumption on the part of the broadcasting business that scientifically recognized findings should disqualify an eminent person from adjudicating an issue pertinent to his professional work created sharp hostility among social and behavioral scientists. In effect, the broadcasters drew a battle line where none was necessary.

Well-known communications scholar Leo Bogart, in a thorough review of the more than 20 separate studies financed by the $1 million, argued that sufficient evidence on the issue of causation had been compiled prior to the Surgeon General's study. He was wrong. The laboratory-type experiments had established the possibility of a real-life causal link between violent portrayals and aggressiveness, and had established some of the factors on which it would be contingent, by demonstrating causation within the artificial confines of the experimental setting. What the Surgeon General's study added was a new component—evidence that everyday viewing of violence was associated with a greater degree of everyday aggressiveness.

This new evidence came from several sources. In a number of samples from various parts of the country, teenagers higher in the viewing of violence were found also to be higher in aggressiveness toward peers, based on the reports of those peers themselves. In another instance, a team of psychologists led by Monroe Lefkowitz and Leonard Eron were able to obtain new data on the television viewing and aggressiveness of several hundred upstate New York teenagers on whom they had collected such data a decade earlier. They interpreted their data as establishing that greater viewing of violent programming in earlier childhood resulted in greater aggressiveness, as measured by the reports of peers, 10 years later. This conclusion rested on a number of assumptions regarding the measures employed and the mode of statistical analysis, but even a harshly critical view left unchallenged the documentation of a positive association, for whatever reason, between the viewing of violent programming in early years and enhanced aggressiveness in later years.

Despite the evidence from laboratory-type experiments, the absence of a positive association between the viewing of violent programming and aggressiveness in data reflecting everyday circumstances would have strongly favored the view that the experimental findings, while real enough, were specific to the experimental setting. The experimental setting differs from the ordinary course of things by the brevity of viewing, the frequent use of specially tailored film, the unfamiliarity of the environment, the presence of an experimenter whose expectations may be subtly communicated to the subjects and thereby shape their behavior, the measurement of effects immediately after viewing without any intervening experience or communication, and the far from general circumstance in which aggressive or destructive behavior will definitely escape retaliation or reprimand. These factors make the experiment extremely sensitive to effects that might not occur in everyday life.

There were several possible interpretations for the positive association reflecting viewing and aggressiveness as they occurred in real life:

1. The viewing could be the result of initially more aggressive persons seeking out violent entertainment; this would amount to a true relationship spurious for inferring an influence of violence-viewing on aggressiveness.
2. The association between the two could be attributable to their shared positive relationship to some third variable; this would amount to a spurious relationship invalid for causal inference regarding violence-viewing and aggressiveness.
3. The aggressiveness could be at least in part the result of the exposure to a greater quantity of violent entertainment; this would constitute a true relationship reflecting a contribution by violence-viewing to aggressiveness.

The strength of the Surgeon General's inquiry is that it helped to evaluate these alternatives. In several samples, the declared preferences, in the sense of favorite programs, as well as the actual viewing of the respondents were recorded. If the association was attributable to more aggressive youths finding unusual satisfaction in violent programming, it would be expected that preference for violence would be equally or more strongly associated with aggressiveness than the viewing of such programming. This did not turn out to be the case. Preference for violence was far more weakly associated with aggressiveness than was the exposure to violence. This finding strongly reduced the plausibility of that explanation. Furthermore, the relationship between exposure to violence and aggressiveness was not significantly reduced when a variety of third variables were taken into account. For example, it would be plausible to expect that youths performing more poorly in school might seek escape in violent programming and might also in frustration be more aggressive. It would also be plausible for youths from families of lower socioeconomic status to be exposed to more violent programming because they view more television and also, because of the norms for their social strata, to behave more aggressively. Neither proved to explain the association between the viewing of violence and aggressiveness. Nor was the association attributable to the attraction of males, whom society encourages to behave more aggressively than it does females, to action and adventure programming. Third variables taken into account included school achievement, intelligence, socioeconomic status, race, and sex. Although in principle the number of third variables that might provide an explanation is infinite, these variables are not only of obvious likelihood but themselves would incorporate—by their own likely substantial relationship with many of the unmeasured variables—a sizable quantity of any unconsidered influence. The fact that these third variables failed to offer an explanation strongly reduced the possibility that factors other than the exposure to violence were at work.

Thus, the combination of the evidence from laboratory-type experiments, which permit causal inference, and from surveys reflecting everyday events, which provide evidence of real-life association and help to eliminate alternative explanations for its occurrence, *together* strongly support the hypothesis that the viewing of violent entertainment increases the likelihood of aggressiveness. However, Bogart, one of those blackballed by the broadcasters possibly as much for his close association with the American Newspaper Publishers Association as for his well-known *The Age of Television*, was certainly correct that the experiments provided presumptive if less than completely persuasive evidence—not only because of the repeated demonstration of causation within their restricted settings, but because they explicate a psychology of the dynamics responsible for such an effect that commands respect for its coherence and plausibility. The hypothesis, then, draws support from three sources: the combined evidence of experiments and of surveys and the explanatory framework developed through the experimentation.

Research has continued on the influence of violent entertainment on behavior; there are studies that do not report evidence of any relationship, but they dictate caution over the extremity or universality of effects and not the rejection of the likelihood of a contribution to aggressiveness. Two investigators, Stanley Milgram and R. Lance Shotland, conducted a series of imaginative field experiments in New York in which persons who had seen in a preview theater either one or another episode of *Medical Center* featuring the theft of money from a plastic charity contribution box or an episode devoid of such an incident later found themselves in a midtown office where they were presented with an opportunity to commit a similar theft. They had been invited to the office to pick up a radio as a reward *but of course!*

for evaluating the episode they had seen, and while a frustrating sign in the empty office announcing that the radios had already been given away increased thefts from a U.S.S. Hope hospital ship charity container, exposure to an episode containing the theft had no influence. Similarly, the actual broadcasting in Chicago, Detroit, and New York, of the story, which included an abusive telephone call from a bar by a drunk to a telethon charity solicitor, did not increase obscene or abusive calls in response to a U.S.S. Hope solicitation appended to the program. In the first instance, the criterion of committing a crime is so severe that, even with several hundred subjects, measurable influence would imply that each evening's programming would ignite emulative crime sprees the next day — and positive findings would have inspired wonderment that such a funny coincidence between programming and lawlessness had escaped notice. In the second instance, the charity solicitation produced fewer than 300 calls in all three cities, including the showing intended to produce baseline data by being bereft of the preceding display of telephonic abuse, a rate demonstrating that the emotionality often inspired by telethons was absent and the null results consequently extremely limited in generalizability. What this research compellingly demonstrates is what Bandura has emphasized so articulately in discussing the experiments in which violent portrayals have increased subsequent aggressiveness: The vicarious experience provided by television and films instructs viewers in the techniques for aggression and antisocial behavior and occasionally may stimulate such action, but behavior is very strongly under the influence of real-life experience, including actual frustration, past success or failure with the class of behavior in question, expectations of efficacy, the state of emotional arousal, and the estimation of risk, retaliation, or punishment. The media do not inscribe a tabula rasa.

Canadian sociologist F. Scott Andison tabulated all the individual studies he could find in which exposure to violent television or film portrayals and aggressiveness were measured. A large majority of the 67 studies—which included laboratory-type experiments, field experiments, and surveys reflecting everyday activity—reported a positive association between exposure and behavior. Whether aggressiveness was measured by imitation, electric shock delivery, or ratings by peers; whether the subjects were nursery school children or of college age; whichever method was employed—the results were preponderantly positive.

The pattern, however, was less strong for the results from surveys than for those from laboratory-type experiments. In part, this may reflect the norms and history of psychology, for experiments with null results are more likely to go unsubmitted or unaccepted for publication, and psychologists as a whole have been particularly interested in the violence-causes-aggression hypothesis and intuitively may have selected portrayals especially likely to produce the outcome anticipated. Both would augment the preponderance of positive experimental results. Undoubtedly, it also reflects the fact that media influence in everyday life is highly contingent on circumstances, and in many instances the requisite configuration of factors will not be present.

It can be expected that a few laboratory-type experiments will fail to produce any relationship between subsequent aggressiveness and exposure to a violent portrayal, and that a few will demonstrate that exposure to a violent portrayal can reduce aggressiveness, because there are probably circumstances under which one or the other would occur—as exemplified by the apparent role of inhibition in reducing aggressive imagery in the early experiment by Feshbach. It can also be expected that surveys will more frequently fail to record a relationship between exposure to violence and aggressiveness because of the many variegated and confounding influences that impinge upon individuals as they go about their daily lives that are curtailed within experiments.

Television is ubiquitous in American life, so persons studied are never those exposed and unexposed to a particular kind of content. In laboratory-type experiments, this influence, as well as that from other sources, is constrained by the proximity to exposure in time and space of the measurement of effects. There is no such proximity in surveys, and thus no such constraint. In everyday life, people invariably have greater and lesser degrees of exposure to violent programming, but the differential exposure may not be sufficient in impact to alter behavior even if individuals within the population under study are being regularly and transiently affected in the manner demonstrated by laboratory-type experiments. In addition, any influence of the media continually will be open to diminution as well as amplification by circumstances.

Such mixed results are illustrated in the two recent longitudinal studies conducted by sociologists and sponsored by NBC and CBS. In a meticulous investigation covering several years in two American cities, J. Ronald Milavsky, an NBC vice-president, found scant relationship between quantity of prior exposure to violent programming and aggressive interpersonal behavior among elementary school boys. William Belson, under the sponsorship of CBS, examined the real-life viewing and behavior of teenage delinquents in England and concluded that the commission of crimes and the infliction of frightful pain could be attributed to the viewing of violent television programming. At present, the results of the laboratory-type experiments, the psychology of behavioral effects which they support, and the mixed pattern of results for surveys encourage the interpretation of null outcomes in some surveys as intriguing but socially welcome qualifications to the belief that the viewing of violence facilitates aggressive behavior in real life. It is crucial, however, that we do not thoughtlessly accept a way of thinking that precludes revision when such revision is dictated by the facts. Surveys with null results, as do experiments with results contrary to the violence-causes-aggression hypothesis, impose the continuing responsibility to examine assiduously their possible methodological superiority—for it is always conceivable that the positive outcomes accumulated to date are artifactual. To err is human; in the social and behavioral sciences, to acknowledge error is sublime, if abrasive to the ego.

The field experiment, in which the control possible in the laboratory-type experiment is ostensibly transferred to a real-life setting without loss of the inferential power to reach conclusions about cause and effect, was long thought to offer a solution to the problem of determining whether exposure to violent programming has any influence in everyday circumstances. The difficulty is that such investigations often fail to match convincingly the very factors that make laboratory-type experiments informative. The Milgram and Shotland field experiments failed to be compelling because of their insensitivity. In other instances, real-life conditions have made it only feasible to use existing groups, such as intact classes, thereby sacrificing the randomization of subjects and the accompanying equality of subjects in various conditions on which causal inference in experiments depends. In other cases, the experimental manipulation itself very possibly has had an effect quite apart from the television stimuli under scrutiny that, unhappily, cannot be disentangled from it. Independent field experiments were conducted by Feshbach and Robert Singer and by William Wells in various residential homes for boys, and the results taken in conjunction suggest that when a no- or low-violence condition is contrived by denying youth the violent programming to which they are accustomed without convincing reason, the frustration induced on its own inspires aggressive behavior. The effect is to mask any increased aggressiveness among those viewing a large quantity of violent programming. As it happens, the pattern of outcomes for field experiments is the same as for surveys—mixed—but on the whole favor the proposition that television violence contributes to viewer aggressiveness, and at present these mixed results merit the same interpretation as do those from surveys.

This is not to say that field experiments in communications are not useful; rather, it is to warn that they are so likely to flirt with methodological peril that their results must be examined with particular care, and that they are not an easy solution to the problem of inferring real-life effects of the mass media. That they can be effective when their risks are overcome is demonstrated by the experience with nursery school children of three psychologists, Faye Steuer, James Applefield, and Rodney Smith. They showed violent and nonviolent Saturday morning programs with animated and live characters to matched groups of five children each in the nursery school setting, a circumstance that evaded frustrating those in the nonviolent group by denying them something to which they were accustomed. Then the researchers observed the interpersonal aggressiveness of the children while at play and compared the behavior with that behavior displayed in identical play circumstances when no films had been shown. This maneuver overcame the onus of experimental artificiality that might be imputed if behavior were assessed in a simulated or unnaturalistic environment, as well as providing a baseline reflecting ordinary play in the absence of television exposure. The children who saw the violent programming engaged in much more physical interpersonal aggression than did those who saw the nonviolent programming. The experiment did not demonstrate that all children in the violent program condition were equally affected, for much of the aggression may have been either retaliatory or emulative of the way other children were behaving, but it did demonstrate that under everyday circumstances exposure to the type of violent programming broadcast on Saturday morning can alter the way children behave. The small number of subjects obviously justifies some skepticism over the equality of the two groups, and the results are not as convincing as they would be were the number greater. However, the point is that the paradigm of the laboratory-type experiment can be artfully elaborated into a field experiment with the inferential benefits of a naturalistic setting.

Susan Hearold, an educational researcher, undertook an ambitious statistical aggregation of 230 experiments and surveys. Her analysis, besides including many more studies than did Andison's, reflects results based on three times as many individuals (more than 100,000), and focused on the degree instead of the direction of the reported relationships. She extracted 1,043 combinations of varying television and film exposure and behavior. Each permitted the comparison of the behavior of persons differing in exposure. She then assessed the degree to which behavior differed in association with media experience by calculating, in each instance, a metric representing the difference in behavior accompanying a difference in exposure. She concluded that in these 230 studies exposure to antisocial portrayals was associated with antisocial behavior to a degree only somewhat less than the apparent beneficial influence empirically documented for educational and medical interventions and instructional programming, such as *Sesame Street* and *The Electric Company*. Exposure to pro-social portrayals were associated with pro-social behavior to a degree somewhat greater than what has been recorded for such interventions. Antisocial behavior was positively associated with antisocial portrayals and negatively associated with pro-social portrayals, suggesting that the former encouraged and the latter inhibited such behavior. Pro-social behavior was positively associated with pro-social portrayals, but unassociated with antisocial or neutral portrayals, suggesting that whatever capacity these portrayals had to arouse viewers to action did not translate into positive behavior of the kind measured.

There was not much difference between boys and girls of nursery school age in the degree of behavior associated with exposure to antisocial portrayals, whether the measure in question was antisocial behavior, a broad category, or the narrower one of physical aggression. For both boys and girls there was a decline for both measures, with exposure associated with lessened degrees of behavior, through ages 10-12, when there were increases among males but continuing declines among the females. This age and sex pattern is much more pronounced for physical aggression than for antisocial behavior in general, and probably reflects changes in socializing experiences and the inculcation of norms—first, the increasing restraints on behavior introduced by parents and schooling and, second, the influence of the differing norms for male and female behavior. Hearold's analysis confirms the presence of sex differences and the importance of norms as a factor on which media effects are contingent, but her aggregation of findings suggests that among very young children such differences are not as common as the many experiments by Bandura and colleagues—in which boys typically have displayed a greater degree of aggressiveness than girls—would have led one to believe, probably for the very good reason that young children have not yet learned the norms peculiar to being a male or a female.

When the portrayals were classified by their verisimilitude in representing everyday entertainment, in contrast to television stimuli especially prepared for laboratory use, pro-social portrayals continued to be associated with a greater degree of pro-social behavior than were antisocial portrayals with antisocial behavior. However, for portrayals of both greater and lesser verisimilitude to entertainment, the association between portrayals and behavior was much more dependent in the pro-social case on the measured behavior paralleling what had been portrayed than was so for antisocial portrayals. This tends to confirm the view that antisocial portrayals may encourage a wide range of antisocial behavior, while pro-social portrayals are more confined to influencing behavior similar to that depicted. The especially prepared stimuli were associated with a greater degree of behavior of whatever kind, reinforcing the belief that artful calculation in production can enhance the social influence of television. A further implication is that pro-social portrayals court failure if the specific behavior depicted cannot be applied by a viewer.

The Hearold analysis leads to three inescapable impressions: First, television and film can have as powerful a measurable influence on immediate behavior as can most interventions intended to alter behavior. Second, television and film can have beneficial effects, particularly when designed to do so and when they focus on behavior that a young viewer is likely to find opportune or applicable in his environment. Third, entertainment, although expectedly not as powerful as portrayals concocted to have a particular effect, is not ineffectual.

The Surgeon General's advisory committee, despite the sizable representation associated with broadcasting, concluded in its report *Television and Growing Up: The Impact of Televised Violence* that the convergence of findings from dissimilar methods—laboratory-type experiments, field experiments, and surveys—supported the hypothesis that violent programming increases the likelihood of aggressiveness among young viewers. Nothing has occurred since to make anyone think differently.

What the research to date does not tell us is the extent or degree to which violent programming may contribute to crime or serious antisocial behavior. The use of an act of crime as the dependent variable in a study imposes an unrealistic criterion for the number of subjects and scope of any investigation, as the Milgram and Shotland study illustrates. The broadcast of Rod Serling's made-for-television movie, *The Doomsday Flight*, has been followed abruptly by increases in airline bomb threats that appear inexplicable except as the consequence of the influence of the program. Newspaper accounts hold that violent attacks on other humans ensued from attackers having seen the garish New York gang movie *The Warriors* or a late-night theater Kung Fu film festival. Since these films portray violence as an adventuresome escapade without the emotional or repulsive physical consequences depicted in *Easy Rider* or *Taxi Driver*, they would certainly seem to fit the conditions advanced by experiment-based theory as facilitative of such behavior. However, we must acknowledge that severe outbursts conceivably attributable to some degree to media effects are so rare as to be outside the feasible reach of scientific inquiry. Criminals often report that they acquired ideas for the commission of crimes from television, but that hardly amounts to scientific verification of such influence. What we are faced with, then, is a question essentially beyond science. If we are skeptical of successive occurrences outside the experimental paradigm, newspaper accounts, and what criminals say, we can have no more in the way of evidence than that provided by the studies of television and film portrayals and aggressiveness, which is certainly consistent with but cannot, by itself, be said to unambiguously support the view that violent entertainment contributes to crime and violence against others.

COMMERCIALS

The average child views about 20,000 television commercials a year—the equivalent of about three hours per week of continuous viewing.

About 10 percent of these accompany programming intended for children, and are correctly thought of as directed at the child audience. Of course, "viewing" as a term does not presume attention, but whatever discount one applies, the amount of exposure to commercials is substantial.

Because children seem to be denied the knowledge of selfish intent at birth, their innocence raises a number of interesting issues. Children learn about advertising as they do everything else—as they grow up. They are presumably incapable until some age of acting with wisdom in behalf of their welfare. Modern literature is filled with accounts of the failure of this social policy told from the perspective of the ward, but it is difficult to deny its validity entirely. The law recognizes their special status by imposing requirements on their behavior, barring some behavior, assigning certain responsibilities to others, and exempting them from commitments that would be binding on adults. Children must receive some degree of formal education; adults are empowered to compel or prohibit their behavior (although not always with success); and until some specific age is reached they cannot be held to contracts to which they affix their signatures. Liquor, beer, and wine cannot be sold to children. As a corollary, commericals become a proper concern of public policy in regard to possibly detrimental or inappropriate influence on children.

Three issues in particular have become prominent. The first is whether the advertising of sugar-coated, fast-, and other manufactured food products encourages children to act contrary to their own health. The second is whether the fact that children do not understand the purpose of advertising until some age implies deception, and thereby harm. The third is whether the creation of knowledge of and desire for various products whose purchase and consumption may be at some variance with the desires of parents imposes undue hardship on the exercise of parental responsibilities.

These issues apply in principle to commercials throughout the broadcasting schedule, but in particular to those accompanying Saturday morning and other programming designed for children. The economic stakes are very high. Some estimates place the potential loss of revenues to broadcasting as high as $45 million annually if two proposed remedies were adopted: banning advertising to children under the age of eight and banning the advertising of heavily sugared products to children under the age of 12. Of course, such a figure may overestimate the eventual impact by ignoring the new advertising for permitted products that might enter the market with the reduction in the pricing of advertising space on children's programming that presumably would follow excising a sizable portion of its present clientele. Certainly the problem of identifying the programming that would fall under such restrictions would be a troublesome one, for the only solution would be a set of formulas based on the recorded audience during some particular period, with an arbitrary stipulation as to the quantity—proportionately or in absolute numbers—of young viewers judged to constitute a population large enough to be classified as constituting an unacceptable degree of jeopardy by exposure to commercials. The demographic makeup of the audience would certainly remain quite stable for the same hour when all outlets are broadcasting a given schedule, but as the hour of broadcast and competing schedules change, so certainly will demographics. In addition, if the restrictions gave broadcasters an incentive to skim the audience by appealing strongly to one age segment and not another, we might find not only rapid fluctuations in demographics but the irony of a new devotion by broadcasters to narrowly age-specific programming, now rejected because it would reduce the size and thus the value of the audience to advertisers, designed to assemble an audience defined as an appropriate target for advertising. Programming for younger children would become the minimum necessary to appease the FCC; older children, the only really valued viewers. The principle of differentiating policy by viewer age is well established in both the scheduling practices of the broadcasting business and in the stance of the FCC that children are an audience requiring special treatment. What is problematical in this instance is the execution.

It also has been argued that certain television advertising accompanying adult programming has a detrimental effect by encouraging the harmful or hazardous use of drugs, beverages, and other products. Commercials for over-the-counter remedies, such as aspirin and antihistamines, have been said to stimulate excessive consumption of such drugs and the use of illegal or quasi-legal substances, such as marijuana. Commercials for beer and wine have been said to stimulate consumption of these and other alcoholic beverages to excess or before attainment of the age of legal access. Such claims raise questions very uncomfortable to examine, for in each case the advertised category of merchandise is recognized as one that is widely used in excess of the boundaries of individual health by adults, yet can be advertised because judicious consumption is redeemed by pleasure or benefit. We are left with the issues of whether the redemptive qualities justify the risk of abuse by anyone, whether young viewers can exercise the expected restraint and judiciousness, and whether such advertising viewed when young may hamper judgment in later years.

In the case of cigarettes, the answers of the society were no, no, and yes. Advertising of a legal product on television was certified by Congress as not benign.

It has also been argued that the depiction of various products—drugs, pesticides, household cleansers, tools, and appliances—encourages their dangerous use in play. The exasperating safety tops on prescription drugs are intended to preclude such application, but over-the-counter drugs do not always carry such protection. Drain cleaners, saws and drills, ovens, ranges, and mixing devices that can burn or trap hair and limbs become threats when used in play. The issue raised here, as with other advertising accompanying programming aimed at adults, is the degree of caution and safeguards required by the substantial number of children in the audience throughout the broadcast schedule, but particularly from late in the afternoon through late evening.

Television advertising and children became a contentious topic early in the 1970s as various citizen groups began to raise such issues through proselytization of the public, complaints to broadcasters, and petitions filed with the Federal Communications Commission and the Federal Trade Commission. The two groups most prominent in this endeavor have been Action for Children's Television and the Council on Children, Media, and Merchandising. The investigation of advertising practices on Saturday morning and during other programming directed at children initiated by the FTC in 1978 is merely the most visible punctuation mark yet in what is certain to be a scenario of continuing disputation and policy formulation.

The effort to restrict the quantity and content of television advertising directed at children has raised another issue—the authority and proper means of financing television for children. The broadcasters, the companies who advertise, and the advertising business assert that restrictions on the quantity of advertising, or restrictions on the content that would severely delimit what could be advertised, would reduce the amount and quality of such programming. If so, not only would these businesses be affected, but so would the various production companies and their writers, directors, animators, and actors. This is an issue on which New York and Los Angeles can agree. The advocacy groups argue that the demand for time on children's programming is great enough so that many restrictions can be imposed without seriously affecting total revenues to broadcasting and advertising, and that the FCC can require broadcasters to program in behalf of children as part of their public service obligation.

The FTC in the past has confined itself to ruling against practices diverging from standards generally applicable to advertising on a case-by-case basis. The broadcasters and advertisers, through codes applied at the network or at the national level by the NAB and the Council of Better Business Bureaus, have attempted to preclude such intervention by adjusting to public complaints, translating specific rulings into more general prohibitions, and preempting regulation by adroitly addressing issues prior to its application. Their position, in essence, has been that any legal product can be advertised if it is not misrepresented or clearly harmful—prohibitions that they hold have been adequately enforced by law and federal regulation as well as their own codes. The FCC has long maintained that it has the power to limit throughout the broadcast schedule nonprogram material, which includes paid-for commercials, promotions for other programming, and public service announcements. However, its impetus to exercise this presumed right, and thereby to subject it to court test, became a gesture confined to theory when the broadcasters, many years ago, confronted the FCC's sole step in this direction with sufficient strength in Congress to counter any such action with a statute stripping the agency of the requisite power. *Sic transit* regulatory intention.

Over the years, numerous changes in the advertising accompanying children's programming have emerged from the dynamics of citizen advocacy, federal regulatory prowess, and self-regulation. Vitamin advertising has been banned by federal fiat; the various codes, incorporating the thrust of rulings and public opinion, bar the delivery of commercial messages by a human or animated character featured in the accompanying program, require disclaimers about assembly and necessary items not included in the product packaging, caution against exaggeration or comparative claims that might stimulate disappointment, prohibit directing a child to ask his parents for a product, limit the emphasis that can be placed on "free" premiums, require that commercials for food portray consumption in a manner nutritionally sound (such as sugared cereals as part of a breakfast that includes fresh fruit), and otherwise delimit the crassness of commercial enticement. At one time, more minutes per hour could be devoted to advertising during Saturday morning and other children's programming than could be directed at adults during primetime. The reason was that broadcasting codes permitted more minutes of nonprogram material during the daytime than in primetime, and it had not occurred to anyone that children's programming might be construed as a special case. That, like much else, is no longer the same. Nevertheless, policy almost wholly has consisted of stipulations and elaborations within the framework accepted by the broadcasting and advertising business—and that is the very perspective that has now come under challenge.

Unhappily, from the viewpoint of even rueful concensus among the various parties, none of the issues can be resolved by the empirical evidence available or likely to become available. In every instance, the interjection of values and human judgment will be necessary. Such an impression is confirmed by the review of the evidence compiled for the National Science Foundation by Richard Adler in 1977 and the research since then; research provides information, but not answers.

A concise summary of the evidence is that (1) a large number of children eight years of age and younger do not understand the self-interested, entrepreneurial motive behind commercials in the sense of being able to accurately define a commercial; (2) children learn brand names of products advertised on children's programming and consume large quantities of sugar-coated, fast-, and other food products advertised to attract them; and (3) children make numerous requests of their parents for advertised products, and in the phrase of the NSF report, "disappointment, conflict, and anger" are often experienced by the child when parents deny their requests. Such sweeping treatment escapes negligent imprecision until some criterion is agreed upon in terms of proportions that constitute a rupture in the social fabric requiring repair. A similar question of quantitative eligibility for redress occurs in regard to the television schedule, for so far policy applied to children and advertising has been largely confined to programming intended primarily for children, defined either by the content or by children constituting a majority of the audience—criteria that ignore the very large numbers of children viewing programming intended for adult or general audiences.

There is no doubt that a sizable number of children below some age do not comprehend the nature of a commercial. The advocacy groups and many lawyers argue that lack of such knowledge implies deception. It can also be argued that such an interpretation is misapplied, on the grounds that description in this context takes its meaning from the possibility of the harm deriving from a purchase that would not be made were the advocacy in its behalf understood as self-interested rather than informative. Children so young as to not comprehend commercials rarely have the disposable income to make many purchases; older children and adults have the money to spend, but they also comprehend commercials. Thus, deception, while unavoidable on the dimension of understanding, fails in the view of broadcasters and advertisers to meet the criterion of misleading the viewer into unwise or naive action.

Commercials are effective in proselytizing children. They learn the names of products, and they learn to like and want them. Marvin Goldberg and Gerald Gorn at McGill University's school of management found that favorability and amount of time devoted to a task by which a toy could be earned were increased among 8-11-year-old boys by exposure to a commercial for the toy. John Rossiter and Thomas Robertson at the Wharton School examined the toy preferences of several hundred first- third-, and fifth-grade boys between November and late December when playthings are most frequently advertised on television. By the end of the Christmas season, expressed preferences had shifted in the direction of the advertised items. Other studies similarly confirm the persuasive efficacy among children of the commercials directed to them. Saturday morning has become very profitable for the broadcasters, and sellers are eager to maintain as great a latitude as possible in employing it and other children's programming as vehicles for their messages.

The argument of inherent deception implies the banning of commercials from television declared on some basis to appeal particularly to very young children. If that argument is not accepted, however, the facts about the efficacy of commercials provide little guidance for policy. Commercials, when assessed individually, usually can be shown to be persuasive, but repetitive exposure seems to be limited in effect to ensuring rememberance of product names that otherwise might be forgotten. Repetition does not appear to increase liking for a product. Further limiting the quantity of commercials that can be broadcast would free more time for entertainment and would be conscience-salving, but, like so many remedies of social engineering, such a limitation would probably only have a minor impact on children's behavior. The data thus are consistent with two options in regard to commercials for sugar-coated and other food products ostensibly undesirable—their continuation without quantitative restriction on the grounds that emphasis on good nutrition will also be persuasively effective, or banning them entirely on the grounds that partial measures will be largely ineffectual.

Parents surely endure numerous requests from children for advertised products. Refusal undoubtedly often disrupts family tranquillity, and no disciple of Julia Child can remain unmoved when a child shouts across the supermarket aisle that some brand of sliced, gooey bread, no matter how nutritionally enriched, is the best in the world. Yet it is far from clear that such events are properly the concern of public policy. As the broadcasters and advertisers have argued, no recognized psychological or social pathology is involved, and the children's requests occur in the context of increased consumption of packaged and fast-foods by adults so that their affinity for such products is not deviant but consistent with social and consumer trends. At the same time, the health of the young remains a legitimate concern of social policy, so the question regresses to the basic one of the circumstances in which a legal product merits specific restrictions on the manner in which it can be marketed.

There is no empirical evidence on the influence on children of beer and wine commercials accompanying general audience programming, although at least one Senate hearing has been devoted to the topic. The evidence available is not consistent with the view that television advertising for over-the-counter drugs, which is not permitted on children's programming, encourages use of quasi-legal and illegal substances. The NBC study conducted by Milavsky that tried to document a relationship between exposure to violent programming and aggressiveness also was able to examine exposure to over-the-counter drug commercials and subsequent drug use. There was no relationship between such exposure and use of quasi-legal and illegal drugs and a very modest positive relationship between exposure and consumption of over-the-counter drugs. Whether this latter relationship represents abuse is moot because symptomatology was not taken into account; the greater use may represent ingestion of the drugs to relieve appropriate discomfort, or it may—in part, at least—represent ingestion unjustified by symptoms. Thus, the drug data are ambiguous about abuse of products as a consequence of exposure to advertisements.

There have been no studies that by scientific standards could link the viewing of commercials for cleansers, pesticides, tools, appliances, and other products with their widespread use in dangerous play, but press reports certainly document that such instances occur. The various codes, as well as the penalities that might be imposed by the civil courts in response to claims of injured parties, inveigh against appeals that would promote endangerment. The remaining policy options would seem limited to more stringent preventive standards, the restriction of commercials for products with apparent risk to hours when children in the audience are at a minimum, or the barring of such commercials altogether. Again, there is a regression to basic issues—when should marketing be restrained and how many children are too many?

As children begin to comprehend the nature of commercials, they also become more like adults in being skeptical and critical of them. There appears to be a very slight positive association between the increase in such reactions as children grow older and resistance to the persuasiveness of advertising. Yet, as anyone can see from the behavior of adults, under-standing and skepticism in regard to advertising do not render it ineffec-tive. The proposed remedy of banning all commercials from programming appealing in particular, by whatever criteria, to children eight years of age and under would appear to safeguard them less by precluding deception than by eliminating exposure. Such a supposition, of course, has no bearing on the ethical propriety of directing advertising at the young.

There are many uncertainties in the various data. Comprehension so far has largely been measured by verbalization, but it could be argued that children can adequately distinguish commercials as sales attempts from the programs they accompany before they are old enough to express or accede to such understanding verbally. Parents apparently think that is the case, for the estimated age when the nature of commercials becomes understood is much lower when based on parental judgments of their children than on the children's own response. Thus, the age at which a remedy is necessary is in dispute as well as whether one is required at all.

Some would make much of the fact that the frequency of children's requests for products advertised on television has not been clearly linked to exposure to commercials advertising those products. Admittedly, other influences could be involved—parents, peers, supermarket displays, or advertising in other media. However, even the most conservative approach would assign a fairly prominent role to television: given the amount of time children expend on it; its status as the medium to which they principally pay attention; and the practical irrelevance of whether its influence is direct, filtered through key peers, or depends on reinforcing what has been learned elsewhere. In this case, if the behavior merits remedy, then television is a plausible point of application.

SOCIALIZATION

Because the psychology on which the behavioral influence of television and film rests is not specific to violence, by analogy it would be expected that socially desirable and constructive behavior, as well as aggressive and antisocial behavior, can be encouraged by its portrayal. Numerous studies support such a view. Yet, such behavior is in itself different enough that the outcome of viewing is not likely to be precisely parallel to that for violence even though the psychology in both cases is the same.

The principle of disinhibition, illustrated in the violence experiments, also applies to behavior that is ordinary. Fear may constrain children from acting freely or easily; the inhibiting reactions to the stimuli responsible can be reduced by exposure to portrayals that cast these stimuli in a less anxiety-producing light. Bandura and Menlove, for example, exposed children who were frightened of dogs either to a series of portrayals in which children first approached and then played freely with a dog or to films of Disneyland and Marineland. The children who vicariously experienced the play with the dog became more willing to engage in such behavior themselves. Rita Poulos and Emily Davidson, also psychologists, similarly showed children said by parents to be afraid of the dentist a film in which an eight-year-old boy fearlessly climbs into a dentist's chair while a fearful four-year-old girl watches. Gradually, the girl loses her fear and climbs into the chair. Children viewing such a portrayal subsequently expressed greater willingness to visit a dentist. Similar results have been reported in regard to snakes and to joining other children in play. One implication, of course, is that entertainment that exploits rather widespread fearfulness of bees, dogs, birds, spiders, cats, and other creatures many of us would prefer to keep at a distance reinforces phobias.

Other laboratory-type experiments have examined the influence on children of portrayals of delayed gratification, deviation from stated rules, sharing, and generosity. The findings conform to what we would expect from the violence experiments. Portrayals increase the likelihood of identical or similar behavior when the portrayed behavior is depicted as successful, rewarding, acceptable, or not leading to punishment. Verbal exhortations can combine with portrayed behavior to increase the effectiveness of a portrayal, but, unlike the example of behavior, alone they are seldom influential.

These experiments and those concerned with phobias, as were some of the violence experiments, employed specially prepared television or film stimuli. The implication that entertainment can promote the various kinds of behavior involved, however, is supported by studies of actual television programming. *Mister Rogers' Neighborhood, Sesame Street,* and *Fat Albert and the Cosby Kids* have been demonstrated variously to increase understanding and knowledge about positive kinds of behavior and, in some instances, to stimulate such behavior itself.

However, the experience of Eli Rubinstein and his colleagues cautions against expecting too much from entertainment. They showed children either an episode of *The Brady Bunch* or one or another of two different *Lassie* episodes. In one, a boy risked his life to save an endangered puppy; in the other, dogs received their usual favorable treatment, but no heroism was displayed in their behalf. After viewing one of these three programs, the children played a button-pushing game in which they could amass points to win prizes. At the same time, they were told that they should pay heed should they hear barking over the intercom, because it would mean that puppies in a distant kennel were in trouble. If they heard such barking, they were asked to push a button that would signal help. The children who saw the *Lassie* episode in which the puppy was saved gave the help signal far more persistently.

In this instance, a portrayal of beneficent intervention stimulated not only helping behavior but self-sacrifice in relinquishing the points that could have been collected by pursuing the game. However, it is important to recognize that the effect depended on the congruence of the televised example and the real-life opportunity to extend assistance. In an earlier experiment, the investigators had found that an example of helping in a portrayal had no effect when the circumstances were quite different from those portrayed. Thus, they turned to an act of assistance that crudely paralleled what had been vicariously experienced. The implication is that entertainment that portrays examples of desirable behavior is limited in influence to circumstances much like those depicted—which simply reinforces the belief that portrayals depend for influence on their apparent relevance to real life.

There are very good reasons to think that in the short run violence may have a stronger influence on aggressive and antisocial behavior than portrayals of more constructive kinds of behavior have on their subsequent performance; but in the long run, the contribution of both kinds of portrayals to constructive behavior probably increases. Anti- and pro-social behavior, to contrast acts that disrupt or promote peaceful human interaction, are not quite symmetrical in character. Thus, the same theory does not predict the same outcome for their portrayal. Antisocial behavior often involves physical acts of aggression with applicability to a wide range of circumstances, exemplified by the sad fact that the time always appears ripe for a child to kick someone. Pro-social behavior often involves rather abstract concepts in which the physical act is secondary to the motive or extremely specific—generosity, helpfulness, sharing, cooperation, and other such notions take on reality in behavior that by itself is very limited in application. A kick is everywhere expressive; mouth-to-mouth resuscitation or rescuing an infant from a traffic island requires a victim of drowning or traffic and a child. The arousal hypothesis (which attributes behavioral influence to the excitatory capacity of portrayals) alone would predict some advantage for violent portrayals in affecting behavior, although not necessarily aggressive behavior if some other kind of action were appropriate or the sole choice, since these portrayals have an inherent edge only blunted by their frequent stereotyping for inducing excitement, and the kind of emotionality induced by other kinds of portrayals intuitively seems less likely to impel action. Children apparently are quite attentive to fast action, so violence also may enjoy superior exposure. The asymmetry in social approval suggests that, while a portrayal in accord with specific motives and interests may help channel them into action, violent portrayals also may be effective precisely because they teach a lesson counter to that of parents and teachers, while pro-social portrayals by themselves may have scant influence because such behavior has reached the maximum possible through proselytization and encouragement. Portrayals certainly are likely to be powerful when they further dispositions already present, but also when they provide information that is new, and particularly when they do both.

These factors favor violent programming affecting aggression in real life over the benign or constructive influence of any kind of content, pro-social or violent. However, there is also good reason to believe that positive influence at least gains in advantage with the passage of time. Children probably become less aroused and, given the redundancy, probably progressively less instructed by the ritualistic violence typical of some television and some movies. As they mature, they become better able to understand the motives behind and the consequences of behavior and the abstract categories which embrace specific acts. It is plausible to think that the more positive lessons of television entertainment embedded in plot and the repetition of varied examples of positive action which, one-by-one, at the time have little relevance increasingly come to have some influence. Such positive effects would hinge not only on increasing comprehension of pro-social portrayals, but also on increased understanding of the pro-social messages that undeniably are part of much violent programming. However, there is no reason to anticipate the termination of antisocial effects, for not all violence will be sufficiently stereotyped to fail to arouse, some new lessons in the application of aggression are likely to be conveyed, and the teenage years present the first opportunity for the application of much that earlier would have been learned from violent programming.

Children could be presumed to acquire most of their information about public affairs from television simply because they watch so much of it and so seldom, even when able, read newspapers or newsmagazines. The empirical evidence supports such a view, while at the same time severely limiting the kind of authority that should be attributed to television. Howard Tolley, Jr., an educational sociologist, surveyed more than 2,500 children seven to 15 years of age in Maryland, New Jersey, and New York about their knowledge of the Vietnam war. His findings constitute a *precis* of the evidence as a whole. Television was far more often named as a source than newspapers, news-magazines, teachers, or parents. Children who watched television news regularly were factually better informed about the war. Newspaper reading also was factually informative, but seldom occurred. Newspaper reading, however, increased the factual knowledge of those already better informed by regularly viewing television news. Parents appeared to have a strong influence on both partisanship and media use. Children tended to take the same ideological stance toward the war as they perceived their parents taking, regardless of their perception of the stance of the newscasters. In addition, children of parents perceived as having an interest in the war were more likely to watch television news regularly. In brief, television informed, parents shaped opinions, and parental interest gave children an impetus toward or exposure to greater amounts of information.

Television has been largely and probably foolishly ignored as a factor in political socialization. The reason is that political scientists have adhered to the model of partisan stability supported by studies on voting conducted in the 1940s and 1950s in regard to children. Political behavior seemed to be pretty much explained by family voting history, socioeconomic status, religious affiliation, ethnicity, and rural or urban residence. There was simply not much left that could be attributed to the media. Television very possibly has altered this situation, partly because it introduced a new element and partly because it functions in a changed context.

Television is different from other mass media in regard to children because children are devoted television patrons. It inevitably deals with some public issues, particularly those involving criminal justice and national security, in comedy and drama. In addition, the young are likely to get most of their news from television, which will certainly be their introduction to the very concept of reportorial coverage. Television news also appears to hold considerable authority among children. Jack Lyle and Heidi Hoffman, two communications researchers, queried several hundred Los Angeles children and found that about three-fourths of those of elementary school age believed that "if you saw it on TV news" it was certain to be true. By high school, the credibility of television coverage is far more frequently questioned. But there is something more to television news than simply the exposure to events, the enlarged vicarious participation in politics, or the trust it inspires. The schools emphasize in their treatment of public events consensual symbols—the office of the presidency, the role of Congress and the Supreme Court, and such abstract questions as the relative merits of bi- and unicameral legislatures. Television, like all news media, emphasizes the dissensual—protests, riots, strikes, the tearful Congressman contemplating an embezzler's cell, the disgraced president stepping into a helicopter on his way to San Clemente. Television is not redundant to what children learn elsewhere, and what it portrays is a world of conflict and dishonesty that often may leave them uncomfortable with their vaguely formulated convictions. Cynicism, skepticism, the belief that not all is right or just—television news inevitably encourages such reactions among the young.

Television also reaches a child whose family is politically unlike families several decades ago. The decline in allegiance to political parties and the increasing number of voters who switch parties between elections and within a ballot that have occurred among adults means that there is less stability to be passed on to children. One result is that the media, and particularly television, come to play a greater role, both indirectly through the information and impressions they bring to parents and directly by what they convey to children. The fact that children appear to follow the partisanship of parents on issues does not imply that television is uninfluential; only that it principally serves as the source of new information that becomes translated into ideology rather than of prefabricated attitudes.

It seems very likely that there is a transitional age when adult media habits become shaped. In elementary school, news viewing very often is the by-product of watching entertainment. As children enter high school, news viewing becomes more frequently independent of other viewing, and the reading of newspapers and newsmagazines increases. At the same time, television viewing as a whole is decreasing somewhat. The shifts reflect so many factors that a summary both comprehensive and succinct is impossible—changes in what is taught as well as in what the child wants to think about, the pull of friends and the lure of adventure that newly take the child from the television set, the belief that more adultlike responsibilities are at hand—but together they suggest that the pattern adopted by the child at this time in regard to the news may continue for many years simply because no period comparable in the magnitude of adjustment occurs earlier or will occur again.

There are probably analogous periods when tastes and preferences for entertainment and artistic endeavor are formed. Himmelweit has been able to obtain data on several hundred young men in the original 1951 English sample in later years, thereby constructing a longitudinal study of media usage covering behavior in the early teens, the mid-20s, and the early 30s.

In a brilliant and very sensitive analysis, she concludes that where tastes differ at any time from what is normative for an age group they prefigure similar tastes later. Consumption of television and other mass entertainment that appeals to a widely varying, heterogeneous audience is apparently not only inversely associated with education and income, but is positively associated with a personal outlook that is marked by an acceptance of the status quo, little interest in the shape that society will take in the future, and feelings of powerlessness. Reading and television viewing, although each has many correlates, are themselves unrelated in enjoyment, indicating that the response of a person to one medium implies nothing about the response to other media. Whenever tastes were observed when they were not common for the peer group—sports, when others were disinterested, or high-brow reading—such preferences proved to be relatively enduring. The implications go beyond the obvious one that taste in entertainment and the arts conforms both to social convention and personal interest. The young person whose interest and perhaps passion are captured by something through parents, teachers, a friend, or by accidental encounter will continue to pursue such inclinations later in life. Taste, which flows toward television out of intellectual and aesthetic passivity of the young, can also be drawn away from television.

These findings, as well as everyday experience, suggest a strong potential role for parents and teachers in regard to the influence of television and other mass media. Parents and probably teachers can shape the opinions that rest on and are elaborated by the information supplied by the media. They can probably shape tastes in directions that are more personal and, since mass entertainment widely attended to by peers is typically less valued than that which deviates from convention and is more particular to the individual, more satisfying. In the surveys of television viewing and aggressiveness, the positive relationship between exposure to violent programming and aggression is reduced when parents discourage or deemphasize such behavior as a means of resolving conflicts. In the laboratory-type experiments, the presence of an adult in the setting in which aggression is measured, or criticism of the portrayed behavior voiced by the somewhat authoritative experimenter, which would symbolize the possibility of social disapproval or punishment, reduces the degree of aggression displayed. Television is quite properly considered a major agent of socialization, but these findings reinforce the view that parents, teachers, and other adults can intervene very effectively in the communication that flows from television to the child.

6

IMPACT OF TELEVISION

The empirical investigation of the role of television in American society has confirmed what many surmised, as well as occasionally documenting what many feared. Its message is essentially one of power, although power whose observable influence is frequently subtle. Television has changed the way Americans live, and to think of it otherwise would be myopic. Like the searing light that interrogators use to extract a confession, television has become an unavoidable and unremitting factor in shaping what we are and what we will become. It is the master of the public eye, an actor among the family, yet it is intricately entwined in the braid of life, so much so that it is easy to mistake it for an entirely passive servant. What is most striking about television is that its power is exercised almost beyond the control of anyone—viewer, celebrity, anchorman, writer, producer, actor, or network executive.

THE UNAVOIDABLE DICHOTOMY

The varying emphases on the public at large and on the individual in assessing the impact of television on America inevitably raises the question of the comparative validity of sociology and psychology. The partisan of one or another inevitably speaks with a forked tongue, for each has its advantages and disadvantages for a particular issue. At the level of the simple explanation of the way people behave, one translates readily into the other. Social factors, even of the broadest magnitude, can hardly affect thought and behavior unless they impinge on the individual consciousness. Political upheavals, economic hard times, the opinions of friends, and the demands of fatherhood, doctoring, or janitoring enter the personal filter described by such concepts as anxiety, expectation, perception, reinforcement, and cognition. Conversely, the makeup of these components for any individual is the product of the behavior of people as a group, class, or society, and much of that to which the individual psyche must respond is determined by the character of these entities. This character is not sensibly construed as the sum of the attributes of the individuals encompassed, but derives from the particular pattern exemplified by the collectivity in question. Psyche, the individual, is governed by the social, whose force is expressed not simply in numbers but primarily in the relationships among those who make up that number.

This exchange between the individual and the social entities among which he moves occurs whether we think in terms of such abstractions as attitudes, values, and beliefs or something so concrete as the behavior in a particular instance of a single person. Such abstractions are a property of the person, the group, and the society; an infinite number of them, which we reduce to a more manageable quantity in deference to our limited powers of comprehension, equal at any moment the individual as well as the social collectivities that constitute his human world. In shifting from the concrete to the abstract, we do not escape from the interaction that occurs constantly between a single psyche and its social environment. We instead merely shift from complex wholes, persons, groups, and societies to the elements into which they can artificially be dissembled. What is constant is that the specific and the singular are never freed from the collective.

Psychology and sociology exemplify the unavoidable dichotomy of focusing either on the individual or on a social entity. Obviously, television, like the automobile, industrialization, fascism, and democracy, can be comprehended only from both perspectives. The same dichotomy applies to the many other modes of thought and investigation on which we must call. For example, child development as a field emphasizes the individual; political science can be roughly grouped with sociology. The dichotomy is absurd if seen as separating truth from error, but it is real enough in distinguishing different bodies of knowledge.

The two approaches can be readily reconciled when we think about the behavior and thought of people, for one leads soon to the other. Partisanship nevertheless remains justified because the approaches serve different ends and identify problems and issues that are not at all the same. A focus on the social leads to questions of the homogenization of culture; changes in the conduct of politics; alterations in leisure; and—on a more intimate level of human interaction—to arrangements that typify parenting, family life, socialization, and the relationships that develop among couples. A focus on the individual leads to questions of learning; specific decisions about purchases, politics, and behavior; and the internal processes of mind and response on which these are contingent. The two approaches also lead to somewhat different strategies of reform or prescription, for apart from

changing programming itself, the one leads to a concern with the institutions that can complement, supplement, or counter the influence of
television, while the other leads more directly to a clinical concern with
the welfare of the individual.

Broadcasters, although they study and think about their audiences in
the mass, in fact approach them, as British sociologist Denis McQuail once
pointed out, as if they were operating "a large laboratory in which millions
of volunteer subjects are exposed to calculated stimuli designed to maxi-
mize the length of stay of subjects and hence the income of the laboratory." Thus, the difference between the approaches lies not in the quantity of persons assessed or in the mode of investigation, but in the theories
that are introduced to explain phenomena and in the concepts which these
theories employ. It is a difference that resides in the eye and mind of the
beholder.

McQuail perceived media research as plagued by an "inconsistency of
vision," with the perspective of television as "a social-cultural phenomenon produced by, and in turn shaping, the history of America" in conflict
and largely incompatible with the frequent treatment of television as "a
mass consumption industry to be described in marketing terms." He is
correct, and correct too in the implication that broadcasters on the whole
have not cared much about the first, which from their perspective has for
them been a decidedly secondary role. What must be added to McQuail's
formulation is that it is also a set of recurring stimuli constantly impinging
on and sometimes affecting the individual in a way that can best be
understood in terms of the psyche. Again, the two poles, the sociological
and the psychological, although inevitably in some opposition, must not
be allowed to distract us totally from one or the other.

What we must confront in thinking about television is a constant
duality of vision. We must examine the glass not only from above but from
below. Otherwise, we shall be like the three blind men who each reached
out for a different part of the elephant and came to three wrong conclusions about the beast.

ATTENTION

The most obvious contribution of television to American life is the
absorption of time that otherwise would be spent differently. By taking
time away from other activities, it has changed the character and availability of other options as well as coloring the way each day is lived out in
the average home. The attention to the mass media for which television is
responsible represents one of the defining characteristics of life in the
second half of our century. The mass media, in entertainment and in news,

have their own language that is often, if not invariably, pared of intellectual depth, subtlety, or the essence of human experience. They are inherently exploitative, sometimes of the best in us, but more often of something considerably less than that. Television serves curiosity, the will to experience and understand, the longing to enter the imaginary, the impulse to engage the imagination and the mind in something that is real enough yet distant enough from everyday life to strengthen and enrich them; but it also serves materialism, vulgarity, the reduction of life to simple motives and single dimensions, and the urge to flee from ourselves and those about us. E.M. Forster once wrote that the "secret casket" of Joseph Conrad's genius contained not a jewel but "a vapor." Nothing half so kind could be said about television. There is neither at the heart of television, and much of mass media, but something closer to an unpopped kernel of corn. Television has made the particular kind of secondary experience represented by the media an integral part of our lives, from a brief period after birth to death—an achievement that was beyond the printing press, the phonograph, the radio, or the movie camera.

Television has not only changed the way politics are conducted and made entertainment in its manufactured form a more prominent part of life, but it has also created, in the likes of Walter Cronkite and Farrah Fawcett-Majors, a new galaxy of heroes and heroines. In many ways, they are no different from those who captured public admiration and passion in the more primitive days of the media—the trench-coated foreign correspondents with the recurring bylines from European capitals and revolutions, the great stars of Hollywood, the idolized bandleaders and singers. Yet, there are certain shifts that suggest that what we have is not more of the same multiplied, but a phenomenon that is in essence new. Just as the television series derived from the movie *Alice Doesn't Live Here Anymore,* the situation comedy *Alice,* embodies little of the gentle realism and compassion of the original, any more than the hand of General Obregon, lost in battle and now enshrined beside Avenida Insurgentes in Mexico City, matches the man in life, the celebrities of television represent a further distillation of the public personage. No longer does public acclaim rest on deeds; instead, it is the product of mere presence in our living rooms. This change amounts to another evolutionary step in the quality of our vicarious participation in life. Television seldom leaves us breathless. It is by turns charming, amusing, diverting, and occasionally compelling, but the singular thrust by which it has held the attention of its subjects has been through orderly, dependable repetition. Marshall McLuhan has made much of the immense degree to which the medium has increased our use of the visual in comprehending the world, and psychologists have emphasized the degree to which it has made vicarious experience a source of influence, but another dimension of television is its implicit celebration of the mundane and the ordinary. The men and women of the media once could be said to be larger than life; now they more nearly approximate our neighbors.

There may be little on earth that is new since the garden gate closed behind Adam and Eve, but there are colorations and tonalities that have not been seen or heard before. These modular celebrities are more insistently with us than their predecessors. They not only are at hand daily or weekly when they perform, but the medium constantly repackages them for use in transient passages, with entertainers a mainstay of talk-shows. Hedda Hopper and Louella Parsons, lionesses of an extinct journalism, laid bare the sins of the stars and kept readers abreast of movieland, but the contribution of television has been to translate this observation of the gods and goddesses into the giddy coverage of *People* and *Us*. The genius of this supermarket journalism is to treat people as characters in sitcom, an approach not available to those who might have thought to apply the principles of Hollywood comedy to journalism because they lacked not only the distilled genre but the cultivation of taste achieved by snapshot television comedy and the talk shows.

Just as attention goes to the Four Seasons while the bulk of the American dining-out dollar goes to fast foods and their variants in steak-and-salad-bar and theme restaurants evoking religious orders, sailing ships, and railroad yards, television has made its most striking claims on the public in its deviations from the routine. These occur when television can take advantage of a naturally occurring event which it can treat as a spectacle. The Kennedy funerals were sombre; the coronation of Queen Elizabeth II a pageant; the visit of Sadat to Israel a high drama; the presidential debates a civics lesson; the Academy Awards a ritual. What they have in common is the attraction of an abnormal number of viewers for an event that television translates through its treatment into a performance. These phenomena represent a cessation of normal activity for a sizable proportion of the public. Empirically, they can be defined precisely as the conjunction of an actual event, television coverage, and an atypically constituted portion of the potential audience. In their impact on society, they take three quite different directions. In the case of the political conventions, the attention of television has changed the event itself. Television in this instance meddles with the symbols of history. In the case of the moon landings, television contributes to a common experience on which the whole society will draw for years to come. The medium in this instance acts as an integrative influence in the society, as it does so often in its everyday programming. In the case of certain other events, television presents an event that appeals disproportionately to a certain

segment of the audience, as the diplomatic adventure in Jerusalem undoubtedly did to the Jewish community. In these cases, television takes on
the less typical role of cultivating cultural variation and differences within
the larger society.

Entertainment and sports also occasionally achieve temporary peaks of
attention that break the normal pattern. These departures from the ordinary levels of attention also vary in the degree to which they provide a
common experience for the disparate segments of society or nurture the
variation that exists. *Roots*, the Super Bowl, and the Kentucky Derby
exemplify television events that cross the boundaries that make groups
distinct. However intensely personal the viewing of such national celebrations may be, they also constitute the symbols by which people express a
common interest and on which social cohesion rests. The documentary
King, which attracted only a minute proportion of white households while
drawing an astounding two-thirds of black households, in contrast culti-
vated the differences by which groups express their identity.

Whether these media events represent fiction, fact, drama, or sport is
irrelevant; they take their social importance from their reformulation of
the ordinary television audience, and by that step make a contribution to
national experience. Yet, in the character of their influence they should
not be taken as unique. The same distinction, to a lesser degree, can be
made for the rest of television. Soap operas and daytime game shows, with
their predominantly female audiences, and *Saturday Night Live*, which
attracts the young and irreverent, cultivate existing differences within the
society; primetime television, and especially situation comedies with their
near-universal appeal, provide a common, unifying experience.

The attention that television commands has reached into streams of
American life far less broad than the currents of entertainment, child
rearing, politics, and leisure. Communications scholar George Gerbner has
pointed out that religion, education, and mass media are all systems by
which the public is acculturated, or introduced to the norms, conventions,
and taboos of society. What sets religion and mass media apart from
schooling is their continuing, repetitious presence throughout life.

One might expect that the great quantity of time consumed by television would infringe on time devoted to religion. The comparison of time
use by television set owners and nonowners in various societies at a time
when set ownership was far from universal suggests that television slightly
reduced the amount of time per week devoted to conventional religious
observance. A more readily visible effect in the United States is the
televising of religious services, most of which rely upon ecclesiastics with
exceptional forensic skill and visible show biz flair. The Sunday morning
audience, when many of these religious broadcasts occur, averages more

than 13 million adults. This underestimates the number of individuals viewing particular programs, because it is the average per minute and viewers tune out to be replaced by new viewers. This is a sizable audience, although certainly minor compared with the 70 million viewing during early primetime. Much of this Sunday viewing appears to be solitary, for the average adult audience per viewing household is 1.04 compared with 1.51 for that primetime period. It is almost equally male and female, contrary to the 25 percent more females than males in early primetime, and surprisingly it is not noticeably older. Whether this is an exact picture of the audience for religious television is uncertain, because it may be distorted by the other programming in the same time period, but it is the best approximation we have. What is less certain is the meaning to be attached to the phenomenon of religious television. Surely some viewers are persons who find it difficult or impossible to attend a local service, or can find none to their taste, while others presumably choose television in place of the service they would otherwise attend. Whether the net effect is an addition or reduction in the number attending religious services is unknown, but certainly the slight reduction in religious observance associated worldwide with the introduction of television has been at least somewhat offset by these broadcasts. It is probable that some viewers are solely adherents of television religion, and the availability of local services is irrelevant. The escalation of dramaturgy in television religion probably alters the demands and expectations of some viewers in regard to what is satisfactory in sermonry.

What does seem clear is that in the case of cultures in which traditional religious observances have a visible and important place, television is one of the central components of modernization that channel public energies toward secular pursuits. Elihu Katz and Michael Gurevitch have documented this phenomenon in Israel by tracing the changes in religion and leisure over the years subsequent to the introduction of television. Television viewing not only conformed to the expected pattern of taking patronage away from other media and other leisure activities, but appeared to be part of a drift away from participation in celebrations and activities associated with Jewish religious practice. The prime symbol of this shift was the Sabbath itself; television broadcasting, initially prohibited during this period, in response to public demand eventually came to be part of the Sabbath as on any other day.

Gerbner suggests that television in the United States can be looked upon as an institution that has assumed some of the functions of a dominant religion, and thus might be thought of as the successor to conventional religion. This is an intriguing perspective. The television business, of course, represents a concentration of economic power, as historically does religion, but economic power is common to many institutions. Where television particularly resembles religion is that the basis of this power is the acceptance of its communications by the intended audience. Television also would appear to resemble religion in the communication of values and interpretation of the world. Television does not do so explicitly as does religion (except in religious and other exhortatory programming), but implicitly. It has been argued by Gerbner and his colleague Larry Gross with great plausibility that television drama as a whole presents, through its violence, a text on the attributes associated with success, power, and dominance, and, through the high frequency with which persons fall victim, another on the hostile and dangerous nature of the world. Similarly, the attributes of figures chosen to appear as entertainers, newscasters, or the subjects of interviews in a favorable context are implicitly identified as the equipment of prominence and success. Television inherently presents winners, and winners represent values.

The connection does not end with the common dissemination of values. Television also establishes a mechanism for the giving or withholding of status. Television's preeminent figures function much like priests in guiding those who watch them to people and things fit for their scrutiny. In this respect, television has become an arbiter of acceptability. It is amusing that when CBS news correspondent Charles Kuralt criticized ABC's Barbara Walters for the sentimental and circumspect interview with President and Mrs. Carter shortly before the 1977 inauguration, he characterized Ms. Walters as "the female pope of television" giving benediction to the new secular leader.

Another dark eddy into which television sometimes enters is terrorism and acts rooted in the outrage of their perpetrators that sometimes horrify but nevertheless fascinate the public. In Haskell Wexler's fact-based film about the 1968 Democratic convention in Chicago, *Medium Cool* (Paramount, 1969), street demonstrators chant, "The whole world is watching! The whole world is watching!" while being filmed by television news crews. On February 2, 1968, NBC televised in color the assassination on a Saigon street of an unarmed prisoner of war by a South Vietnam general. Some consider the reaction to this four minutes of footage to be the turning point toward public opposition to the war. These two incidents focus our attention on the possible effects on subsequent events of particulary dramatic television news coverage.

One of the apparent phenomena of modern life is the tendency of terrorist acts and outbreaks of violence of a particular kind to occur in a series. One suspects that if such events were plotted in a time series there would be a tendency for those similar in character to cluster together. If so, one factor is probably the coverage given these events by the mass

P Phillips

media. It would be silly to hold television responsible apart from other mass media—newspapers, radio, and news magazines. This is not solely because these other media also disseminate information about such events, but because the values expressed in television news are derived largely from the values of journalism as a whole, although clearly modified by the particular demands of television as a medium. Nevertheless, it is possible that in certain instances television may have a particularly strong role in any such effect.

Television coverage is our preeminent symbol of public attention, and reportage of one event may encourage similar acts because of the apparent assurance of subsequent attention from the medium. At the same time, television coverage may provide helpful clues for the commission of antisocial acts. Its often vivid camera portrayals supply concrete examples of daring, a sense of actuality, and a realism, which by themselves may not only be instructive, but may serve as the compelling axis around which the typically more detailed and inevitably drier accounts of newspapers and magazines will be organized and assigned enhanced meaning by potential perpetrators. The increase in airline bomb threats apparently attributable to *The Doomsday Flight* television film gives credence to such a view.

Television coverage may also be a factor on which the unfolding of events is contingent. Television coverage occasionally is a condition for safe treatment of hostages or the conduct of negotiations. The access to public attention implied by television may distort the decision-making and behavior of those involved. The concept of all the world as a stage is heightened by television coverage. In some cases, it may restrain behavior by the apparent guarantee of exposure to public scrutiny. In others, it may exacerbate dreadful events by giving participants a sense of playing roles in high drama.

Crime probably exceeds terrorism in its susceptibility to influence by the mass media both because it is so much more dependent on individual circumstance and because the opportunities for its commission are ever present. Unresolved political tensions, although common enough, are far less common than greed or personal desperation. Banks, gas stations, and supermarkets are everywhere. In those incidents in which hostages are taken, the media—particularly television because it so often transmits events directly to the public—may become a central element in their resolution, for men act differently when their deeds are on public display. Television enjoys an advantage over other media not only for the superior instruction of its visual depiction but because, unlike the case with politically motivated terrorism, it may be the sole medium reaching many potential perpetrators. In the language of psychology, the successful bank robbery is no more than a portrayal of rewarded antisocial behavior, and we should not be surprised if such stories encourage emulation. Epidemics of crime may sometimes be the chance conjunction of independent events, but they also may constitute a chain whose links are fashioned by the very attention focused on such behavior.

"The whole world is watching!" Television coverage may be a calculated outcome rather than the concomitant of organized displays of dissatisfaction and unrest. Apart from its symbolic value in representing the achievement of public attention, there is the actual political worth of the fact of attention. It is a standard tactic for disaffected groups to seek public sympathy through publicity, or to attempt to provoke ruthless reprisals by the flagrant disregard of authority. The first we see regularly; the second is dramatized in the classic pseudodocumentary *The Battle of Algiers*, in which the rebels trap the French into hostile acts that mobilize the non-French population against them. The medium of television probably has raised the stakes in such tactics not only because of its access to the public but because of its immediacy and the visual drama it imparts to the events in question.

Such tactics hinge on the expectations held by perpetrators. Their target may be the masses, or the elite that wields power; they may hope to work through public opinion, or to preempt it through the anticipatory response of those in authority. Exposure of the public to shocking events is the immediate fact, but in the arsenal of political action it is a sword that cuts differently in different circumstances. When General Westmoreland returned from Vietnam after the American defeat, he declared that television's dissemination of the ugliness of war had made war unacceptable to the American people. He had in mind film footage such as the Saigon murder. The detachment imposed by literary convention is undeniably lacking in television coverage; we read and reread the prose of Ernest Hemingway when the events described would hardly give us pleasure unshielded by the cadence of style. Television drama may render violence sane by avoiding its gruesome consequences, but television news in Vietnam stripped all sanity from war. We are right to be skeptical that in consequence war itself has become any the less likely, but that particular war probably became more difficult to prolong. The Saigon murder, like most of the events covered by television, was not designed to serve political goals through the media, but they illustrate the means inherent in television by which such ends may be achieved.

These varied possible outcomes of television coverage stand in contrast to the benefits of an informed public. The rights and privileges of the press rest on the service that it renders the public, and television is in no way dishonored by the power and behavior peculiar to it. What we must recognize is that the price of an unfettered press, which we accept as the surest safeguard for an informed public, is sometimes an outcome unintended and unwelcomed by the press. We would err to accept the myth so compatible with the practice of journalism that news and events are synonymous, with the former reflecting the latter. Events make news, but news also surely makes events, and television news influences events in its particular way—through the behavior it is so well equipped to encourage, through the emotions it so powerfully evokes, and through the anxieties and misgivings on the part of those in authority these powers so often invoke.

FAMILY LIFE

Television has introduced a new set of experiences to the American household quite apart from what is viewed. The films of families viewing television document that attention is commonly discontinuous—people wander in and out of the room, children play and fight, meals are consumed. It would be a mistake, however, to conclude that because television is not often treated as a theater performance it is irrelevant to the life lived around it, for the large number of hours that the set is on each day in the average household makes it the framework within which human interaction occurs.

Less time was devoted to conversation by those who possessed television sets in the multination UNESCO study discussed in Chapter 2. This gives support to the speculation that it reduces interaction among family members, but whether the point of reduction is trivial conversation, the exchange of opinions, play with children, the display of affection, the exchange of confidences, or some other dimension of interpersonal communication is moot. Television also has reduced the time parents devote to child care—by distracting them from their children, by providing an impersonal babysitter, by substituting for the reading of bedtime stories by a mother or father.

Almost half of American households have two or more television sets, and 90 percent of these multiset households have a set in the principal social arena, the living or "family" room. Another 90 percent of these multiset households have the second set in a bedroom and, contrary to the belief that the second set belongs to the children, about 66 percent of these bedroom sets are in adults' bedrooms. Multiple sets in the home are a mark of individual and national affluence, but their effect is to increase the privatization of the television experience and to alter the social aspects of viewing. Viewing alone increases, joint viewing by family members decreases, and the composition of social viewing changes. Joint viewing by husbands and wives alone becomes more common, as does viewing by children with adults not present. The consequence is to further separate adult and child experiences. These effects are a second step in the privatization of experience begun with the apparent declines in conversation and child care.

Nevertheless, family members frequently must decide among themselves on what to view. A fairly consistent composite of the dynamics of this decision-making emerges from several studies. Disagreement is fairly frequent (about half of the time for adult couples and for both parents and children, about three-fourths of the time for mothers and children). When the choice is not mutual, children prevail almost as frequently as adults. In the family, television often has the status of the "children's medium" for which, by reasons of interest and attention, the young have become the acknowledged resident experts.

Otherwise, decisions follow the norms of status and majority rule: Fathers tend to prevail over children and mothers; older children tend to prevail over younger; and among adult couples, males tend to prevail over females. What television has added to family life in this decision-making is a new arena for the delineation of roles and exertion of authority, of which the most striking aspect is the emergence of the young as arbiters of household behavior.

The reshaping of time use by television raises the question of the value of what has been discarded. It was obviously of less worth to those involved than what they have chosen to do instead, and one might expect that the activities most deflated were those at the periphery of people's lives. When television was introduced into England, sociologist William Belson began a study of family life that extended over six years. He discovered that at first many activities were reduced, both in the frequency of engaging in them and in the interest expressed in them, but that after six years had passed these levels were not much below their initial standings. Then he reexamined the trends separately for activities that, prior to television, had been engaged in more and less frequently. The recovery in the less frequent activities was almost perfect after six years, but even after such long habituation the more frequently engaged-in activities remained below their pretelevision levels. This makes sense, for it is the frequent activities that can be reduced without their loss altogether. What television shrinks, then, is not what is peripheral but that which is central to the lives of viewers.

Thus, it is not solely through the introduction into the home of images, statements, and portrayals that television has joined parents, teachers, and the community at large as an agent of socialization. Television has also found a means of influence through the changes it has brought to the way parents behave and to the landscape of habit with which the family confronts the child.

SECONDARY INFLUENCE

The research on the influence of television inevitably places the medium at the forefront of attention. It would be a mistake to transfer a focus that serves the ends of scientific inquiry to our understanding about real-life events. Television is much more sensibly thought of as a secondary rather than a primary influence.

The television business itself made this error in its naming of several persons, some of them of worldwide eminence, as unsuitable for membership on the Surgeon General's scientific advisory committee appointed to examine the television violence issue, and in its assumption over many years on this and other questions of social impact of the posture of the monkey who can hear no evil. Neither, in the light of evidence or of the awkward position in which the business subsequently found itself, was justified. Television in these instances acted with unaccountable insensitivity and fearful anxiety, as if it had never heard of the First Amendment that would safeguard any programming it felt was worthy and had no one to call upon who could place these issues of unintended and unexpected impact in context. It was behavior more understandable in a storekeeper embroiled in a dispute over his contribution to traffic congestion than in a business that not only continually declares its fealty to the public interest—and in fact is charged by statute with such responsibility in the licensing of stations—but also has, because of its very nature as a communications medium as well as its prosperity, access to endless intellectual resources. Alas, one should probably not expect more of the best and brightest here than anywhere else. The acrimony, if not the controversy in entirety, that beset programming in the 1970s could have been avoided had television early and openly acknowledged that violent programming might have deleterious effects.

The irony acquires a sharper edge from the private behavior of the networks, which in their self-regulatory review of programming had always examined particularly graphic portrayals of violence with some care. If offense to public taste was the paramount concern, the possibility of undesirable influence was not entirely ignored. What transpired in the 1970s after the Surgeon General's inquiry was a more ready acknowledgement in public that violent programming might have adverse effects, particularly on children. In the arena of controversy, however, television found itself the legatee of its previous ostrichism. The path it had chosen, which over the years had been marked by unkept promises to reduce violence, now set it at odds with (1) prestigious organizations, such as the American Medical Association and the national Parent-Teachers Association, which demanded a reduction in violence; (2) the writers and producers in Hollywood, who could not fathom an apparent hypocrisy that now demanded conformity to nonviolent programming after so many years of publicly denying that violence was a problem; and (3) the social and behavioral science community, which felt impugned both in regard to the integrity of certain of its prominent members and of the validity of its theories and methods.

It is extraordinary that an institution built upon the manipulation of public behavior should have chosen such a foolish strategy. The psychology of those blocks that spread northwest of Rockefeller Center has always been that of Chicken Little; the sky is seen daily as falling, and the response is usually suited in its judiciousness to the perception. In this case, the decisions were made on business grounds by businessmen with a vision no broader than the scope of much of the programming on which their status rested, and television missed the opportunity for intellectual leadership in the dispassionate assessment of its role in society.

The psychology of behavioral effects does not imply that every portrayal influences a sizable portion of viewers, nor does it imply that effects are wholly detrimental to viewers even though its empirical foundation has been the study of aggressive behavior. It simply posits a set of principles that identify attributes of the television portrayal, the circumstances, and the viewer likely to facilitate or deter effects. The associated evidence of a positive correlation among adolescents between quantity of violent programming viewed and everyday aggressiveness that gives some confidence that the kind of influence demonstrable in the laboratory setting actually occurs in real life certainly should not be interpreted to mean that factors other than television do not have an important and probably superordinate role. The fact that not all surveys in which the viewing of violent programming can be matched against aggressiveness produce positive correlations encourages the view that the occurrence of such behavioral influence to a degree sufficient for detection depends on environmental or social characteristics of the audience that are far from fully understood. The values communicated by parents, and probably by teachers and peers, are important; so, too, probably, are many other factors.

Every society has a set of boundaries beyond which behavior is punished or leads to special treatment in order to minimize disruption and maintain social relations in their current manifestation. The issue that has drawn the most attention in the United States in connection with television has been its possible contribution to delinquency, crime, and other seriously harmful antisocial acts. The evidence supports the proposition that the viewing of television violence increases the likelihood of subsequent aggressiveness on the part of the young, but it does not equally strongly support the proposition that viewing violence increases violations of the law and seriously harmful antisocial acts.

The acceptance of the second proposition is contingent on the assumption that television's demonstrated contribution to aggressiveness augments the frequency of serious transgressions, where behavior would be governed by deeply ingrained inhibitions and fears of punishment or disclosure to shame. Albert Bandura, whose experiments and thoughts have contributed so much to our understanding of the psychology on which any behavioral influence of television rests, places television third behind family and social milieus in which a person resides as a source of influence. He further argues that any actual display of behavior is likely to be strongly dependent on immediate circumstances, such as the perceived likelihood of success and, in the case of aggression, frustration and deprivation. He finds that the consistent expression of any kind of behavior will depend on the reinforcement it receives and how effectively it serves the ends sought by the individual. Such a perspective fits everything we know about human behavior. It is more plausible to argue that seriously harmful or criminal antisocial acts are somewhat shaped by television than that they are very often instigated by it, because such a view accepts the ability of television to enhance capability to perform an act by providing a model without requiring that it overcome major psychological and social restraints. Aggressive or antisocial behavior that falls closer to or within the borders of acceptability is somewhat more likely to be instigated by a portrayal, and far more likely to be shaped by television.

There is not a great deal of evidence aside from *The Doomsday Flight* phenomenon, the anecdotal accounts of prisoners about the sources for some of their techniques, occasional reports in the press, and such flamboyant capers as the museum theft executed by Miami beach boys inspired by the movie *Topkapi* to link television with the commission of seriously harmful or criminal antisocial acts. However, one should not make too much of such sparsity, for the likelihood of such a link—in the sense of irrefutable scientific evidence—being observable is minimal. The sole study focusing on the issue, the field experiments conducted in New York by Stanley Milgram and R. Lance Shotland, found no evidence of a link, but this negative finding is not very persuasive because the rate of antisocial behavior required in this instance for statistical significance was far in excess of that necessary for significant social impact—which would require only the influencing of a minute proportion of viewers. The difficulty with the null effects argument in this context is that it rests on the ability to demonstrate a direct relationship and thereby unrealistically ignores the complexity of human behavior. The variety of factors—individual, situational, and societal—involved in a seriously harmful antisocial act are so many and so intertwined that any direct connection to television is unlikely to be readily demonstrable.

When such circumstances make a direct test implausible, the alternative is to test propostions consistent with the supposedly untestable proposition. This, in effect, is what has occurred in the experiments on violence viewing (which demonstrate a number of ways in which violent portrayals may increase subsequent aggressiveness) and the surveys that provide positive correlations between prior violence viewing and aggressiveness.

It cannot be said with certainty whether the contribution of television violence to seriously harmful antisocial behavior is great, negligible, or null. The evidence, however, is supportive of some contribution—conceivably through increasing the frequency of such acts, but more probably through shaping them.

Several writers—in particular Gerbner and Gross—have argued that television is a powerful reinforcer of the status quo. The ostensible mechanism is the effects of its portrayals on public expectations and perceptions. Television portrayals and particularly violent drama is said to assign roles of authority, power, success, failure, dependence, and vulnerability in a manner that matches the real-life social hierarchy, thereby strengthening that hierarchy by increasing its acknowledgement among the public and by failing to provide positive images for members of social categories occupying a subservient position. Gerbner and Gross have found that heavy television viewers differ consistently from light viewers in perceiving the real world as more similar to the social makeup of television drama. Heavy viewers are more likely to overestimate the proportion of persons engaged in law enforcement, the frequency of violent and criminal acts, and the likelihood of their falling victim to an act of crime or violence. This phenomenon does not seem to be explained by the initial fearfulness of persons to venture from their dwellings, which would increase their hours of proximity to a television set and presumably their viewing, for the distortion occurs for facets of society not plausibly related to crime, such as the proportion of nonwhites in the world and the size of the labor force engaged in such television-popular occupations as health care. Two psychologists, Anthony Doob and Glenn Macdonald, have demonstrated that at least in Toronto the greater fearfulness reported by heavy television viewers is explained by the actual incidence of crime in the neighborhood, for the positive relationship between fearfulness and television viewing that they too observed disappeared when neighborhood crime was taken into account. However, they also found a number of relationships between television viewing and perceptions and beliefs about the world that were not explained by the neighborhood, the source of firsthand impression. These perceptions and beliefs included the frequency of murders in the city and the desirability of keeping a firearm in the home. In addition, the disappearance of the relationship for the sample as a whole is not complete when sites are examined individually. When Doob and

Macdonald examined the data for each of the four combinations of high versus low crime and urban versus suburban sites, they reported that among persons in the urban high-crime area, those who had greater exposure to television violence also expressed greater fearfulness. This opens the possibility that the data in fact specify the site of a relationship and, by implication, the real-life circumstance of heightened risk and legitimate anxiety upon which it is contingent, that is simply less wide in occurrence than Gerbner and Gross originally concluded.

Thus, the possibility that television cultivates a distorted perspective on the world remains, and the inclination to attribute considerable power to the medium is encouraged by the fact that in the data of Gerbner and Gross the distortions entertained by heavy viewers are not consistently eliminated by exposure to the alternative and, in the eyes of some, more fact-based source of the daily newspaper. Gerbner and Gross believe that the status quo derives support not only from the authority and power they argue is implied for those who commit violence, who typically are white males in the prime of life already privileged in the social hierarchy, but also from the kind of distorted outlook that the medium may stimulate, which would seem conducive to support for stricter laws, punitiveness against transgressors, and expanded license for agencies of law enforcement. However, the proposition that television reinforces the status quo inevitably must remain speculative; as Gerbner and Gross observe, the proposition is so holistic that it is somewhat like asking about the effects of Christianity or Confucianism.

There is also the related possibility that continual exposure to violence in entertainment may make viewers less sensitive to violence in real life and as a consequence less ready to assist or intervene when others are hurt or threatened. Psychologists long ago demonstrated that people become progressively less emotionally aroused as they observe someone being tortured. Might not a similar desensitization occur through television viewing? Victor Cline and his colleagues found that children who were heavy television viewers exhibited less physiologically measured emotional arousal when shown a violent portrayal on television. Ronald Drabman and Margaret Thomas asked children to monitor the play of children in another room on a television monitor; they found that when the children who had been asked to be watchful were first exposed to a violent television portrayal they were less quick to summon adult intervention when the children on the monitor became violent. Thomas, Drabman, and two colleagues subsequently found that the physiologically measured arousal or emotionality of 8- to 10-year-old children and of college students induced by televised scenes of real-life violence was lower after they had seen a sequence from a violent police drama than after they had viewed clips of a nonviolent volleyball game. In the case of children, the real-life violence was a fight between two preschoolers; for the college students, news footage of the rioting at the 1968 Democratic national convention. These three studies, one documenting that heavy viewers are somewhat different in their capacity to be aroused, the second identifying exposure to a portrayal as responsible for lessened readiness to intervene, and the third demonstrating reduced reactivity after seeing a violent episode, would appear to support the view that the viewing of television violence is desensitizing. However, what they leave ambiguous is whether the subject of that desensitization is the media or real life. In each case, the violent experience to which the subjects were less responsive was introduced by television itself. We know that the meaning people attach to what they experience depends on cues, and a major cue in these instances was the medium conveying the experience. The evidence is more clearly in support of desensitization toward further media than real-life experience— which, of course, fits the reasonable belief that yesterday's sensation is often today's bore. Conceivably, violent programming reduces sensitivity to the violence actually around us, but it almost certainly dulls our reaction to what we experience in the media. There is a psychological as well as the social explanation of changing norms for increasing emphasis in television and films on violent and sexual encounters, for people need ever-stronger fare to achieve the same degree of pleasurable excitement.

Television certainly provides countless examples of violence, but it also provides countless examples of intervention. Just as televised examples of violence may, by various means, encourage aggressive behavior by a viewer, so too may televised examples of helpful intervention encourage that kind of behavior, for the same psychology applies to both. It is true that violence in entertainment may have the advantage in achieving some impact, but this does not mean that portrayals of constructive behavior are totally ineffectual. It is more plausible to believe that the kind of violent programming common on television, with its rescues and bravery, has increased the likelihood of intervention and decreased the possibility that an incident in real life would traumatize an observer to the point of ineffectuality (although both effects would surely be extremely modest in degree) than to believe that television stands in the way of people helping each other. Nevertheless, the progressive desensitization of taste does imply that television and films will present increasingly vivid portrayals of violence that may contribute to antisocial behavior on the part of some of those in the audience.

One of the attributes of a television society is the historically unprecedented sharing of the same experience. The only comparable sharing prior to television, except for the more limited popularity of radio, were religious and patriotic rites. Although amount of viewing and attitudes toward television vary by social strata, with viewing and favorability of attitude inversely related to education, viewing is sufficiently similar for television to be considered a national experience. Leo Bogart has hypothesized that the consequence, because of television's attachment to the acceptable, is to reduce tolerance of deviation and, because of the emphasis on middle-class values, to assimilate blue-collar and other subgroups to a middle-class perspective.

There is substantial evidence in behalf of the view that television contributes to the way people perceive the world and that the result is a somewhat more commonly held way of thinking and behaving. Belson, for example, found that socioeconomic differences in the activities engaged in by families in England were somewhat reduced once they possessed a television set. In the United States, other investigators have found that turning to television to learn something is markedly more common among those of less education, among the elderly, among the poor, and among blacks. Melvin DeFleur and Lois DeFleur found that beliefs based on television were more uniform among children and parents than those derived from other sources. These varied results combine to give the definite impression that television is homogenizing in its impact. However, it is not at all clear that intolerance can be related to such homogenization.

During its several decades of existence in America, television for many has undeniably broadened by at least occasionally exposing viewers to places, events, and examples of human interaction that they would not otherwise have experienced. It is this very fact that has made it at times offensive and threatening to some. Because of the inevitable allegiance of television to the perspective of the urban, educated class in whose hands it rests, entertainment, sports, and news have encouraged the classic liberal value of tolerance. The process that is justifiably labeled homogenization has lessened, not deepened, traditional ties and convictions, with the result that people have become more rather than less accepting of the behavior of others that they disdain for themselves. Such influence is likely to have been modest in the specific instance or for any individual because of the well-known propensity of people to interpret what they experience in a manner consistent with previously held beliefs. Two separate studies, one by Stuart Surlin, the other by Neil Vidmar and Milton Rokeach, give us an example in regard to *All in the Family*. Caucasian viewers with a substantial degree of ethnic provincialism tended to perceive Archie Bunker as voicing an accurate view of the world, while those less narrow in outlook perceived the liberal son-in-law as correct. Satire failed to penetrate the barrier of conviction, and so surely must other portrayals be halted in what might reasonably be presumed to be their effect. Nevertheless, given the continuing exposure of viewers to unfamiliar experiences and the inculcation of new generations that grow up with television, its influence in a liberalizing direction has probably been profound.

Although there is no way that television can be legitimately identified as the cause, sociologists Theodore Caplow and Howard Bahr found that the adolescents of the midwestern community that Robert and Helen Lynd described in their famous examinations of American social patterns, *Middletown* and *Middletown in Transition*, today are markedly more tolerant of those who think or act differently than adolescents were 50 years ago. What makes this increased tolerance so striking is that religious, political, and social attitudes remained largely unchanged; patriotism, the Protestant ethic, and family and marriage were as honored as they were half a century ago, and there was nothing to support the verdict of so many journalists and social commentators, working on intuition instead of with empirical data, of severe alienation and the desertion of traditional values in the young. Television, which has brought the outside world to middle America, is plausible as a major contributor to this tolerance, a view which Caplow and Bahr share, for they told the New York *Times* that in their opinion television was responsible for this particular and singular transformation.

Television has continued the struggle begun by public education by new means. As we become more alike in what we will permit to others, we may become less kindly disposed toward those who believe everyone should behave and think as they do. Thus, we have come to stand on its head the dictum advanced by Barry Goldwater at the beginning of the 1964 presidential campaign that extremity in behalf of liberty is justified; the prevailing sentiment, reinforced by television, is that extremity is fine if it does not go beyond consenting adults.

The reinforcement of the status quo, homogenization, and assimilation to middle-class values are effects plausible, but admittedly problematic as to their reality, that revolve around the very great heterogeneity of American society. It is this heterogeneity that makes it possible to give credence to the views of Gerbner and Gross, whose argument about the status quo implies some resistance and hostility to deviant behavior, and to the view that television has encouraged a tolerant, liberal outlook.

The point is not simply that such heterogeneity means there is enough variety within the society for every kind of effect, often opposite in direction, to occur, for crosscurrents and eddies are inevitable in any social entity as huge and varied as the United States. The point, easy to lose sight of when looking at these arguments one by one, is that this heterogeneity makes it possible for these three trends to coalesce in the mainstream of influence.

Social distinctions are rooted in education, income, occupation, and ethnic and family background. These are not attributes erased by the adoption either of isolated new values or of a common source of diversion. For all that television has done and might do, the social hierarchy remains—if altered somewhat in its evolution, and quite possibly in significant ways, by television. Homogenization and assimilation to middle-class values, and in particular the acceptance of thought and behavior at variance with one's own, do not represent a diminution of the social hierarchy or a disruption of the status quo, but the reinforcement of the values on which the hierarchy rests. The convergence of perspective that has apparently occurred, and is certainly likely to continue, in fact tempers the hostilities that ordinarily would emanate from social distinctions. Class warfare has never been absent from the American experience, and at times, in monetary and economic disputes, in labor strife, and in ethnic clashes, it has had a prominent role. However, it has not been a defining characteristic of American life or a pervasive condition which Americans have accepted as a basis for their behavior; television has moved us, if ever so slightly, a further step away from such a state of mutual siege.

Yet, in some respects, television also disrupts the social order. It certainly does so through any contribution it may make to acts of crime and violence. By stimulating aggressiveness that falls within the boundaries of acceptability, it also would make the minute social interactions on which the conduct of our lives depends somewhat more sharp and, occasionally, less pleasant. There is an abrasiveness, when we are not too busy watching television itself, for which television probably has some responsibility. By continually exposing at least a portion of its audience to affluence, possessions, and modes of life beyond their economic and social resources, it almost certainly has encouraged dissatisfaction with what American society offers. Some have been alienated, others angered. These feelings sometimes may translate into very constructive behavior, either on the personal or political level, but they also may leave many, with no recourse to solve their predicament, confused and unhappy. By sometimes being manipulated by the dissident few in their attempt to reach the many, and by the exploitation of extremism, social and political, that is the inescapable product of the values by which newscasters select stories from events, television certainly upon occasion exacerbates hostilities within America. The television coverage of the civil rights marches in the South, and later the Vietnam protests, surely aided these causes by drawing support to them, but it also aroused strong feelings among their opponents. When television emphasizes symbols that threaten, as it did in the coverage of antiwhite as contrasted with integrationist groups in the 1960s, it sharpens antagonisms and delays their resolution. Thus, television is two trains running toward a society whose members have more rather than less in common, and toward that society's occasional division and inflammation.

SELF-DETERMINATION

Television in America is a product of the decisions made in the 1930s and before about the role of government in broadcasting, and the three attributes that characterize it so well—nonpaternalism, entertainment, and competition—have their foundation in what took place a half-century ago. One of the silliest of beliefs, encouraged at every turn by those whose business is broadcasting, is that the American system is the only sensible or feasible arrangement. There is much that can be said in its favor, certainly. It has always been a meritocracy in which individual success—whether it is management, station operation, or creative endeavor in production, writing, or acting—has hinged on ability. One is justified, however, in questioning whether popularity and the assembly of a mass audience is a particularly admirable measure of ability. In the commercial broadcasting that so dominates present arrangements, it has been self-supporting. If in regard to public service it has never been profligate, it would be unfair to label it as unremittingly niggardly. Risk, in terms of audience appeal, has not been absent, although it has not been typical. The hunger for profits, visible in so many decisions made by broadcasters, has continually been compromised not only by the statutory requirement of providing public service that is a condition of station licensing but also by the aspirations of those who work in broadcasting. The worldwide popularity of American programming, a by-product of the quantity of material produced for the American market and of the rich production budgets that its lucrativeness has justified, has made a positive if not grand contribution to our balance of payments. We have had the privilege, rare in the world, not only of seeing a national administration conclude that television in its news and public affairs coverage represented a contrary voice, but seeing it powerless to act effectually in its belief. None of these facts, however, should blind us to the simple truth that what we have had in the way of television is something we invented. We might have invented differently.

We have arranged for advertisers to pay directly for our programming, and we pay indirectly by our purchases of products. This has resulted in programming that is acceptable to the many, but seldom extraordinarily attractive to anyone in particular. As Les Brown, the New York *Times* television writer, has said, broadcasters speak of the public as if it were one, but in fact the exchange of time and money that begins with the purchase of advertising time and ends with purchases at the supermarket, department store, fast food outlet, and automobile dealer is based on the continuing attention during primetime of a central segment of the American population who regularly watch television—those cajoled subjects in the endless experiment. The foundation of television's wealth is the minority of heavy viewers who consistently can be shifted back and forth across channels and programs. Television *is* a national experience; it crosses every demographic boundary imaginable, but paradoxically its dependable middle is a passive crowd of onlookers who surpass the A.C. Nielsen Company averages in their weekly attention.

We have been, in all this, somewhat more clever than we had imagined. By placing financial support in the medium's own hands, we have avoided the problem that increasingly confronts those systems dependent on fees levied on viewers. In such systems, the set owner pays the equivalent of a tax, and the problem is inflation. The costs of operating the system inevitably rise more quickly than the revenue from fees, because the levy is a political decision contingent on popular support. People naturally oppose an increase in household expenditure, and politicians are disinclined to oppose them. The result is that these systems are now facing periods of declining ability to serve their audiences as they have in the past. The price of our accidental prescience, and one that we have paid for three decades, is the priority that is given to profits and popularity in programming decisions and the secondary and sometimes entirely absent place occupied by social and artistic conscience.

There will be no need to change the terms by which we describe the basic character of television in America, but over the next two decades television nevertheless will change. Network television certainly will be weakened by the alternative means of dissemination offered by satellites, by the increased programming made available by cable and pay-TV (which now reach less than one in four homes), and by the new latitude that the tape and disc in-home playback systems will give to viewers in treating television with the selectivity formerly possible for books, magazines, recorded music, and theatrical experiences. Television financed by advertising will remain with us. Some price that advertisers will pay willingly can be established for time on any program, however small the audience; thus, any television, including that broadcast on a pay-TV basis, is subject to becoming an advertising vehicle. On the assumption that commercials make a program somewhat less appealing, the question from the viewpoint of the telecommunications businessman who has alternatives is the extent to which he will wish to rely on advertising revenue instead of that from subscriber fees. From the larger perspective of telecommunications as a whole, the question becomes one of the pattern of advertiser-supported, free, broadcast, cable, fee, and in-home playback television that will evolve as each competitor seeks profit maximization.

The networks will remain able to assemble profitable audiences for two reasons. First, many segments of the population will not be able or willing to spend the money that will give them the diversity offered by the new technology. Second, some genuinely popular programming may not fit any other means of dissemination so well as a financial investment. For example, the Olympics are certain to draw a huge audience on broadcast television, but it is not so clear that they would fare nearly as well on a pay-TV basis, even if all homes were equipped for such service. The reason is that the audience for the Olympics, entranced though it becomes by what it sees. is not an audience of impassioned partisans. The audience for team sports, both professional and collegiate, is made up of fans who await confrontations with zeal. This devotion, missing from the motive of those who assemble for the Olympics, ensures a sizable number who will pay to see a 90-yard run.

The new technology that apparently will make so much available to the individual viewer will not necessarily improve television except in the sense that a Big Boy hamburger provides a change from a Big Mac. As the networks grudgingly surrender portions of their audience to programming from other sources, the audience they can offer advertisers will become smaller and, because less affluent, less desirable in composition. Their declining revenues will accelerate competition for viewers, and may very well impel the networks toward sensationalism and the video equivalent of the tabloids that adorn supermarket checkout stands. Such a trend will be encouraged by the increasing predominance in the audience for "free" broadcast television of those with lesser education and intellectual discernment. The sole exception, besides some sports and certain media events certain to draw huge audiences, is likely to be made-for-TV movies, which now command multi-million-dollar budgets and have a degree of polish beyond those of a few years ago. Made-for-TV movies, which have a proven capability to attract very large primetime audiences, may be able to resist incursions on the network audience because of their ability to be accepted as special events. The availability of quality programming from nonnetwork means remains problematic. It is not clear that the audiences that can otherwise be assembled will be large enough to attract enough advertising revenue, or that they will be able or willing to pay enough directly, to support new production. At the same time, the available stock of material—reruns and theater movies—that now seems so plentiful will become increasingly familiar. What once seemed bountiful may eventually become tiresome. We can expect more of the same from the new technology and a greater disparity between the occasional triumphs and obdurate trivia of network television programming.

The new technology also introduces a troubling question of equity. Undeniably, it has the capacity to serve audiences too small to have been of much interest to commercial broadcasters—for example, children of a specific age, ethnic minorities, the elderly, and those seeking education or high culture. Whether it will do so depends on unknowns of economic feasibility. However, if it does, the redemption of the golden promise of television for some will mean the continuing voiding of the claims of others. Households of lower socioeconomic status will have to do without, or with less of whatever is available, because use of cable, pay-TV, video discs, cassettes, and in-home playback and recording is contingent on the ability to pay. For the foreseeable future, the new technology will mean greater inequality in access to entertainment and information. If it in fact does disseminate programming arguably more congruent with the public interest, then many will wonder whether the exclusion of those already less privileged economically is not intolerably in conflict with that interest. Broadcast policy in the United States, however slow, clumsy, or imperfect in execution, has been guided by the principle of maximum public access, and it is that principle which the new technology contravenes. Admittedly, no one has worried much that stage, screen, and recorded music have not been freely available to all, but television is accorded a different status in our society analogous to that of education, where policy is committed to minimizing inequities. The new technology is creating for television the problem that the public library was devised to solve for print media—involuntary exclusion—and it is a problem that will become the more, not the less, disquieting the better the new technology performs in providing programming for interests and motives relatively ignored in the past by the oligopoly of commercial broadcasting. It is the old conundrum the new technology poses so sharply: whether and how to meddle in the evolution of the mass media in behalf of a social idea.

What is easy to overlook is that television itself, from the beginning, has been a technology with its own imperatives. The next two decades will bring a new stage in its evolution in the United States, but there are certain trends that have been observed worldwide that make the American system in some ways the most prominent example of what television inevitably is and will be. Thus, the relationship that American television has to television in other societies is paradoxical. American television stands in contrast in the minor role it has accorded a philosophy of public communication in which popularity has a subordinate place, but illustrates in certain respects the direction in which the technology drives television everywhere, whatever the prevailing philosophy of those who are supposedly its masters.

Television is a costly mass medium that, once in place as a system with production and transmitting facilities and television sets accessible to almost everyone, overcomes every barrier of literacy and isolation that restricts the flow of other media and experience. Radio did much the same, but with the reduced power of an aural medium. Newspapers, books, and magazines were never in the same class in their ability to reach a mass audience. Television's character around the world derives from the twin facts of its enormous reach and ability to communicate. Once television as a system is in place, there is created—from the public and from political leaders—pressures to employ it to the utmost. Thus, the drive toward popularity, toward satisfying the interests of the masses, continually reduces the proportion of programming that can be said to be cultural or directed to a small segment of the audience. At the same time, as television conforms to the appetite of the broadest possible range of the potential audience, the public itself comes to think of it more and more as a medium of triviality and diversion, and to expect and demand less and less from it.

We see everywhere those signs that are so amplified in the American system. There is everywhere on the part of those responsible for television a concern with popularity, so that the high cost of the system can be justified by the attention that the public devotes to it. Everywhere, in communist and socialist as well as in mixed and capitalist societies, the same demographic pattern marks the audience. At one time, when television was novel and the system was not fully in place, certain socialist societies presented a viewing pattern distinct from that of the United States. People of higher socioeconomic status and greater education watched somewhat more hours per week. The reason, of course, was that the programming in that transient stage was proportionately more devoted to culture and information. As the television system became more thoroughly entrenched, programming changed to employ unused hours of broadcast time and to consume the hours unfilled by viewing at the disposal of the public. The demographic pattern soon came to resemble that in the United States. For example, in Russia today, there are not only game shows that emulate the western system at its most trivial (if harmless), but the demographics of the audience match those of the United States—greater viewing by women, the less educated, blue-collar workers, the elderly, and children. In Israel and Australia, a complementary shift has been observed. Broadcasting has not only become more devoted to entertainment, but the people themselves have changed in what they expect from the medium. In both countries, people anticipated much more in the way of cultural enrichment before they saw television first-hand. Once they had spent a few months or years with the medium, their outlook changed. The television experience in our homes is undeniably the product of the system we have established, and different systems will produce different kinds of television, but television as a technology is also in part its own master. In the United States, it has simply been given a particularly free rein.

REFERENCES

CHAPTER 1

Barnouw, Eric. *Tube of plenty: The evolution of American television.* New York: Oxford University Press, 1975.

Brown, Les. *Television: The business behind the box.* New York: Harcourt Brace Jovanovich, 1971.

Cole, Barry, & Oettinger, Mal. *Reluctant regulators.* Reading, MA: Addison-Wesley, 1978.

McGill, William J. et al. *The public trust.* For the Carnegie Commission on the Future of Public Television. New York: Bantam, 1978.

CHAPTER 2

Allen, Charles L. Photographing the TV audience. *Journal of Advertising Research,* 1965, 5, 2-8.

Bechtel, Robert B., Achelpohl, Clark, & Akers, Roger. Correlates between observed behavior and questionnaire responses on television viewing. In E. A. Rubinstein, G. A. Comstock, and J. P. Murray (eds.), *Television and social behavior, vol. 4. Television in day-to-day life: Patterns of use.* Washington, DC: U.S. Government Printing Office.

Bogart, Leo. *The age of television.* New York: Frederick Ungar, 1972.

Bower, Robert T. *Television and the public.* New York: Holt, Rinehart & Winston, 1973.

Frank, Ronald E., & Greenberg, Marshall G. Zooming in on TV audiences. *Psychology Today,* 1979, October, 92-103, 114.

Loye, David, Gorney, Roderic, & Steele, Gary. Effects of television: An experimental field study. *Journal of Communication,* 1977, 27, 206-216.

Meyersohn, Rolf. Leisure and television: A study in compatibility. Doctoral dissertation, Columbia University, 1965.

Robinson, John P. Television and leisure time: Yesterday, today, and (maybe) tomorrow. *Public Opinion Quarterly,* 1969, 33, 210-223.

Robinson, John P. Television's impact on everyday life: Some cross-national evidence. In E. A. Rubinstein, G. A. Comstock, and J. P. Murray (Eds.), *Television and social behavior, vol. 4. Television in day-to-day life: Patterns of use.* Washington, DC: U. S. Government Printing Office, 1972.

Robinson, John P., & Converse, Philip E. The impact of television on mass media usage: A cross-national comparison. In A. Szalai (ed.), *The use of time: Daily activities of urban and suburban populations in twelve countries.* The Hague: Mouton, 1972.

Robinson, John P., Converse, Philip E., & Szalai, Alexander. Everyday life in twelve countries. In A. Szalai (ed.), *The use of time: Daily activities of urban and suburban populations in twelve countries.* The Hague: Mouton, 1972.

Steiner, Gary A. *The people look at television.* New York: Alfred A. Knopf, 1963.

Szalai, Alexander (Ed.). *The use of time: Daily activities of urban and suburban populations in twelve countries.* The Hague: Mouton, 1972.

CHAPTER 3

Clarke, Peter, & Fredin, Eric. Newspapers, television and political reasoning. *Public Opinion Quarterly,* 1978, 42, 143-160.

Dennis, Jack, Chaffee, Steven H., & Choe, Sun Yuel. Impact of the debates upon partisan image and issue voting. In S. Kraus (ed.), *The great debates: Carter us. Ford, 1976.* Bloomington: Indiana University Press, 1979.

Efron, Edith. *The news twisters.* Los Angeles: Nash, 1971.

Emery, Edwin. Changing role of the mass media in American politics. *The Annals of the American Academy of Political and Social Science,* 1976, 427, 84-94.

Epstein, Edward Jay. *News from nowhere.* New York: Random House, 1973.

Eyal, Chaim H. Time frame in agenda-setting research: A study of the conceptual and methodological factors affecting the time frame content of the agenda-setting process. Doctoral dissertation, Syracuse University, 1979.

Frank, Richard. *Message dimensions of television news.* Lexington, MA: Lexington Books, 1973.

Hickey, James. What America thinks of TV's political coverage. *TV Guide,* April 8, 1972, 6-11.

Hofstetter, C. Richard. *Bias in the news.* Columbus: Ohio State University Press, 1976.

Katz, Elihu, & Feldman, Jacob J. The debates in the light of research: A survey of surveys. In S. Kraus (ed.), *The great debates.* Bloomington: Indiana University Press, 1962.

Kraus, Sidney (Ed.). *The great debates: Carter vs. Ford, 1976.* Bloomington: Indiana University Press, 1979.

Lang, Kurt, & Lang, Gladys E. The unique perspective of television and its effects: A pilot study. *American Sociological Review,* 1953, 18, 3-12.

Lazarsfeld, Paul F., & Merton, Robert K. Mass communication, popular taste, and organized social action. In W. Schramm and D. F. Roberts (eds.), *The process and effects of mass communication.* Urbana: University of Illinois Press, 1971.

Lemert, James B. Content duplication by the networks in competing evening broadcasts. *Journalism Quarterly,* 1974, 51, 238-244.

Levy, Mark R. The audience experience with television news. *Journalism Monograph,* 1978, 55, 1-29.

Lucas, William A., & Adams, William C. Talking TV and voter indecision. *Journal of Communication,* 1978, 28, 120-131.

Mendelsohn, Harold A., & Crespi, Irving. *Polls, television and the new politics.* San Francisco: Chandler, 1970.

Mendelsohn, Harold A., & O'Keefe, Garrett J. *The people choose a president: Influences on voter decision making.* New York: Praeger, 1976.

Paletz, David L., & Elson, Martha. Television coverage of presidential conventions: Now you see it, now you don't. *Political Science Quarterly,* 1976, 9, 109-131.

Patterson, Thomas E., & McClure, Robert D. *The unseeing eye.* New York: Putnam, 1976.

Pride, Richard A., & Wamsley, Gary L. Symbol analysis of network coverage of Laos incursion. *Journalism Quarterly,* 1972, 49, 635-640.

Robinson, John P. The audience for national TV news programs. *Public Opinion Quarterly*, 1971, 35, 403-405.

The Roper Organization. *Public perception of television and other mass media: A twenty year review, 1959-1978.* New York: Television Information Office, 1979.

Sears, David O., & Chaffee, Steven H. Uses and effects of the 1976 debates: An overview of empirical studies. In S. Kraus (Ed.), *The great debates: Carter vs. Ford, 1976.* Bloomington; Indiana University Press, 1979.

Shaw, Donald L., & McCombs, Maxwell E. *The emergence of American political issues: The agenda-setting function of the press.* St. Paul, MN: West Publishing, 1977.

Stevenson, Robert L., Eisinger, Richard A., Feinberg, Barry M., & Kotok, Alan B. Untwisting the news twisters: A replication of Efron's study. *Journalism Quarterly*, 1973, 50, 211-219.

CHAPTER 4

Baldwin, Thomas F., & Lewis, Colby. Violence in television: The industry looks at itself. In G. A. Comstock and E. A. Rubinstein (Eds.), *Television and social behavior, vol. 1. Media content and control.* Washington, DC: U.S. Government Printing Office, 1972.

Bandura, Albert. *Aggression: A social learning analysis.* Englewood Cliffs, NJ: Prentice-Hall, 1973.

Bandura, Albert, Ross, Dorothea, & Ross, Sheila A. Imitation of film-mediated aggressive models. *Journal of Abnormal and Social Psychology*, 1963, 66, 3-11. (a)

Bandura, Albert, Ross, Dorothea, & Ross, Sheila A. Vicarious reinforcement and imitative learning. *Journal of Abnormal and Social Psychology*, 1963, 67, 601-607. (b)

Banham, Reyner. *Los Angeles.* New York: Harper & Row, 1971.

Berkowitz, Leonard. Violence in the mass media. In L. Berkowitz, *Aggression: A social psychological analysis.* New York: McGraw-Hill, 1962.

Berkowitz, Leonard, & Rawlings, Edna. Effects of film violence on inhibitions against subsequent aggression. *Journal of Abnormal and Social Psychology*, 1963, 66, 405-412.

Cain, James M. *Double indemnity.* New York: Random House, 1978. (a)

Cain, James M. *The postman always rings twice.* New York: Random House, 1978. (b)

Cain, James M. *Mildred Pierce.* New York: Random House, 1978. (c)

Cantor, Muriel G. *The Hollywood TV producer.* New York: Basic Books, 1971.

Cantor, Muriel G. The role of the producer in choosing children's television content. In G. A. Comstock and E. A. Rubinstein (Eds.), *Television and social behavior, vol. 1. Media content and control.* Washington, DC: U.S. Government Printing Office, 1972.

Chandler, Raymond. *The big sleep.* New York: Ballantine, 1977.

Chandler, Raymond. *The long goodbye.* New York: Random House, 1976.

Coover, Robert. *The origin of the Brunists, A novel.* New York: Bantam, 1979.

DeFleur, Melvin L., & DeFleur, Lois B. The relative contribution of television as a learning source for children's occupational knowledge. *American Sociological Review*, 1967, 32, 777-789.

Didion, Joan. *Play it as it lays.* New York: Bantam, 1971.

Feshbach, Seymour. The stimulating vs. cathartic effects of a vicarious aggressive activity. *Journal of Abnormal and Social Psychology*, 1961, 63, 381-385.

Gaddis, William. *The recognitions, A novel.* New York: Avon, 1974.

Geen, Russell G. The meaning of observed violence: Real vs. fictional violence and consequent effects on aggression and emotional arousal. *Journal of Research in Personality,* 1975, 9, 270-281.

Gerbner, George, & Gross, Larry. Living with television: The violence profile. *Journal of Communication,* 1976, 26, 173-199.

Gerson, Walter M. Mass media socialization behavior: Negro-white differences. *Social Forces,* 1966, 45, 40-50.

Hardwick, Elizabeth. *Sleepless nights.* New York: Random House, 1979.

Heffner, Richard D., & Kramer, Esther H. Network television's environmental content. Rutgers University, 1972. (unpublished)

Klapper, Joseph T. *The effects of mass communication.* New York: Free Press, 1960.

Krull, Robert, & Watt, James H., Jr. Television viewing and aggression: An examination of three models. Presented at the meeting of the International Communication Association, Montreal, April 1973.

Lambert, Gavin. *Slide area.* New York: Dial Press, 1968.

Lurie, Allison. *The nowhere city.* New York: Avon, 1975.

McArthur, Leslie Z., & Resko, Beth G. The portrayal of men and women in American television commercials. *Journal of Social Psychology,* 1971, 97, 209-220.

MacDonald, Ross. *Archer in Hollywood.* New York: Alfred A. Knopf, 1967.

MacDonald, Ross. *The Galton case.* New York: Alfred A. Knopf, 1959.

Mendelsohn, Harold A. *Mass entertainment.* New Haven, CT: College and University Press, 1966.

Tannenbaum, Percy H., & Zillmann, Dolf. Emotional arousal in the facilitation of aggression through communication. In L. Berkowitz (Ed.), *Advances in experimental social psychology, vol. 8.* New York: Academic Press, 1975.

Weidman, Jerome. *I can get it for you wholesale.* New York: Simon and Schuster, 1937.

West, Nathaniel. *The day of the locust.* New York: Bantam, 1975.

Zillman, Dolf. Excitation transfer in communication-mediated aggressive behavior. *Journal of Experimental Social Psychology.* 1971, 7, 419-434.

CHAPTER 5

Adler, Richard (Ed.). *Research on the effects of television advertising on children.* Washington, DC: U.S. Government Printing Office, 1977.

Andison, F. Scott. TV violence and viewer aggression: A cumulation of study results. *Public Opinion Quarterly.* 1977, 41, 314-331.

Bandura, Albert. Social learning theory of aggression. *Journal of Communication,* 1978, 28, 12-29.

Bandura, Albert, & Menlove, Frances. Factors determining vicarious extinction of avoidance behavior through symbolic modeling. *Journal of Personality and Social Psychology,* 1968, 8, 99-108.

Belson, William A. *Television violence and the adolescent boy.* England: Saxon House, Teakfield Limited, 1978.

Bogart, Leo. Warning, the Surgeon General has determined that TV violence is moderately dangerous to your child's mental health. *Public Opinion Quarterly,* 1972, 36, 491-521.

Fesbach, Seymour, & Singer, Robert D. *Television and aggression: An experimental field study.* San Francisco: Jossey-Bass, 1971.

Goldberg, Marvin E., & Gorn, Gerald J. Children's reactions to television advertising: An experimental approach. *Consumer Research,* 1974, 1.

Hearold, Susan L. Meta-analysis of the effects of television on social behavior. Doctoral dissertation, University of Colorado, 1979.

Himmelweit, Hilde T., Oppenheim, A. N., & Vince, Pamela. *Television and the child.* London: Oxford University Press, 1958.

Himmelweit, Hilde T., & Swift, Betty. Continuities and discontinuities in media usage and taste: A longitudinal study. *Journal of Social Issues,* 1976, 32, 133-157.

Lefkowitz, Monroe M., Eron, Leonard D., Walder, Leopold O., & Huesmann, L. Rowell. *Growing up to be violent: A longitudinal study of the development of aggression.* New York: Pergamon, 1977.

Lyle, Jack, & Hoffman, Heidi R. Children's use of television and other media. In E. A. Rubinstein, G. A. Comstock, and J. P. Murray (Eds.), *Television and social behavior, vol. 4. Television in day-to-day life: Patterns of use.* Washington, DC: U.S. Government Printing Office, 1972.

Milavsky, J. Ronald. TV and aggressive behavior of elementary school boys: Eight conceptualizations of TV exposure in search of an effect. Invited address at the meeting of the American Psychological Association, San Francisco, August 29, 1977.

Milgram, Stanley, & Shotland, R. Lance. *Television and antisocial behavior: Field experiments.* New York: Academic Press, 1973.

Poulos, Rita W., & Davidson, Emily S. Effects of a short modeling film on fearful children's attitudes toward the dental situation. State University of New York, Stony Brook, 1975. (unpublished)

Rossiter, John R., & Robertson, Thomas S. Children's TV commercials: Testing the defenses. *Journal of Communication,* 1974, 24, 137-144.

Rubinstein, Eli A., Liebert, Robert M., Neale, John M., & Poulos, Rita W. *Assessing television's influence on children's prosocial behavior.* Stony Brook, NY: Brookdale International Institute, 1974.

Schramm, Wilbur, Lyle, Jack, & Parker, Edwin B. *Television in the lives of our children.* Stanford, CA: Stanford University Press, 1961.

Steuer, Faye B., Applefield, James M., & Smith, Rodney. Televised aggression and the interpersonal aggression of preschool children. *Journal of Experimental Child Psychology,* 1971, 11, 442-447.

Surgeon General's Scientific Advisory Committee on Television and Social Behavior. *Television and growing up: The impact of televised violence.* Report to the Surgeon General, United States Public Health Service. Washington, DC: U.S. Government Printing Office, 1972.

Tolley, Howard, Jr. *Children and war: Political socialization to international conflict.* New York: Teachers College Press, Columbia University, 1973.

Wells, William D. *Television and aggression: Replication of an experimental field study.* Graduate School of Business, University of Chicago, 1973. (unpublished)

CHAPTER 6

Belson, William A. Effects of television on the interests and initiative of adult viewers in Greater London. *British Journal of Psychology,* 1959, 50, 145-158.

Bogart, Leo. American television: A brief survey of research findings. *Journal of Social Issues,* 1962, 18, 36-42.

Bogart, Leo. The mass media and the blue-collar worker. In A. Shostak and W. Gomberg (Eds.), *Blue-collar world: Studies of the American worker.* Englewood Cliffs, NJ: Prentice-Hall, 1965.

Brander, Laurence. *E.M. Forster: A Critical Study.* Lewisburg, PA: Bucknell University Press, 1968.

Brown, Les. *Keeping your eye on television*. New York: Pilgrim Press, 1979.

Caplow, Theodore, & Bahr, Howard M. Half a century of change in adolescent attitudes: Replication of a Middletown survey by the Lynds. *Public Opinion Quarterly*, 1979, 43, 1-17.

Cline, Victor B., Croft, Roger G., & Courrier, Steven. Desensitization of children to television violence. *Journal of Personality and Social Psychology*, 1973, 27, 360-365.

Doob, Anthony N., & Macdonald, Glenn E. Television viewing and fear of victimization: Is the relationship causal? *Journal of Personality and Social Psychology*, 19••, 37, 170-179.

Drabman, Ronald S., & Thomas, Margaret Hanratty. Does media violence increase children's toleration of real-life aggression? *Developmental Psychology*, 1974, 10, 418-421.

Gerbner, George. An institutional approach to mass communications research. In L. Thayer (Ed.), *Communication: Theory and research*. Springfield, IL: Charles C. Thomas, 1967.

Katz, Elihu, & Gurevitch, Michael. *The secularization of leisure*. Cambridge, MA: Harvard University Press, 1976.

Lynd, Robert S., & Lynd, Helen Merrell. *Middletown*. New York: Harcourt Brace Jovanovich, 1929.

Lynd, Robert S., & Lynd, Helen Merrell. *Middletown in transition*. New York: Harcourt Brace Jovanovich, 1937.

McLuhan, Marshall. *Understanding media: The extensions of man*. New York: McGraw-Hill, 1964.

McQuail, Denis. End of an era. *Journal of Communication*, 1979, 29, 227-229.

New York *Times*. "Typical" U.S. town keeps 1920's (sic) values. March 25, 1979.

Surlin, Stuart H. Bigotry on the air and in life: The Archie Bunker case. *Public Telecommunications Review*, 1974, 2, 34-51.

Thomas, Margaret Hanratty, Horton, Robert W., Lippincott, Elaine C., & Drabman, Ronald S. Desensitization to portrayals of real-life aggression as a function of exposure to television violence. *Journal of Personality and Social Psychology*, 1977, 35, 450-458.

Vidmar, Neil, & Rokeach, Milton. Archie Bunker's bigotry: A study in selective perception and exposure. *Journal of Communication*, 1974, 24, 36-47.

ABOUT THE AUTHOR

GEORGE COMSTOCK is S.I. Newhouse Professor of Public Communications at Syracuse University. He was science adviser and senior research coordinator for the Surgeon General's Scientific Advisory Committee on Television and Social Behavior. For several years, Comstock was a senior social psychologist at the Rand Corporation, Santa Monica, California, and is the senior author of *Television and Human Behavior* (Columbia University Press). He holds a Ph.D. and an M.A. from Stanford University and a B.A. from the University of Washington.